The Well-Decorated Cake

TOBA GARRETT

Photographs by **Steven Mark Needham**

Illustrations by Christine Mathews

STERLING PUBLISHING CO., INC.

NEW YORK

Edited, arranged, and layout design by Jeanette Green
Designed by Wanda Kossak and Jeanette Green
Photographs by Steven Mark Needham
Illustrated by Christine Mathews
Assistants to Toba Garrett—Maria McEvoy and Tina Cinelli
All cakes in this book were designed by Toba Garrett

Library of Congress Cataloging-in-Publication Data

Garrett, Toba.
   The well-decorated cake / Toba Garrett ; photographs by Steven Mark
Needham ; illustrated by Christine Mathews.
      p.   cm.
   Includes index.
   ISBN 0-8069-9199-2
   1. Cake decorating.   I. Title.
TX771.2.G37 2003
641.8'653—dc21

2003000291

1 3 5 7 9 10 8 6 4 2
Published in paperback 2004 by Sterling Publishing Co., Inc.
387 Park Avenue South, New York, N.Y. 10016
© 2003 by Toba Garrett
Distributed in Canada by Sterling Publishing
c/o Canadian Manda Group, One Atlantic Avenue, Suite 105
Toronto, Ontario, Canada M6K 3E7
Distributed in Great Britain by Chrysalis Books Group PLC
The Chrysalis Building, Bramley Road, London W10 6SP, England
Distributed in Australia by Capricorn Link (Australia) Pty. Ltd.
P.O. Box 704, Windsor, NSW 2756 Australia
Printed in China
All rights reserved

Sterling ISBN 0-8069-9199-2 Hardcover
ISBN 1-4027-1773-3 Paperback

Photo Acknowledgments: We thank photographer Jeff Harris and *Bride's* magazine for permission to use the
photo (originally with an artistic slant) of Toba Garrett's Monogrammed Wedding Cake, shown on pp. 76
(detail), 78 (detail), 81 (detail), 91, and 126, first published in the magazine's fall 1998 issue. We also thank
photographer Wendell T. Webber and *In Style Weddings,* for permission to use the photo of Toba Garrett's Crystal
Wedding Cake, shown on pp. 8, 102 (detail), and 127, first published in the magazine's spring 2002 issue.

Dedicated to the women in my family who helped shape my culinary path:

My great-grandmother Eliza, the best cook on Edisto Island;

my grandmother Sarah, the best baker on Edisto Island;

grandmother Daisy, the best cook in Vance, South Carolina;

Aunt Henrietta, who showed that simple meals can look and taste delicious,

and Sarah Elizabeth, my mom, who pulled it all together for me.

Special Thanks

Without the generous support and help of these people, this book could not have been written. I owe them all a great deal of thanks and sincere gratitude: Steve Magnuson; John Woodside; Steven Mark Needham; Christine Mathews; Maria McEvoy; Tina Cinelli; Jeanette Green, my editor; and Jeannine Ford, Sterling's design director.

I especially want to thank James Garrett, my husband and partner, who held my hands and kept me centered and focused; our son Phoenix, who taste-tested the recipes; Rick Smilow, president of the Institute of Culinary Education (formerly Peter Kump's New York School of Culinary Arts) for providing space for photo sessions; Mary Bartolini, who is always there; my colleagues in pastry, Cara, Andrea, Michelle, Craig, Faith, Chad, Rebecca, Gerri, Carey, Scott, Melanie, Reeni, Nick, Barbara, and Michael from Florida; my in-laws James and Jean Garrett for their constant support; my sisters Chicquetta and Valerie; my brother Kartrell; and my dad, George Edward, for his undying love.

Contents

Preparing the Perfect Cake

A MASTER CHEF'S SECRETS

A Cake-Decorating Master Class with Toba Garrett

Welcome to the art of cake decorating. As an instructor and culinary artist specializing in cake and cookie design, I'm often asked for hints about creating the well-decorated cake. I believe that the true art of cake decorating rests in the art of piping.

My first cake-decorating book was an eye-opener. The author was Marguerite Pattern and the decorating style was Australian. I bought this book nearly three decades ago even though I didn't yet have the skills to execute the cakes in her book. When I look at this Australian cake-decorating book now, among hundreds of books on decorating and baking, I realize that my first Wilton-based cake-decorating classes and subsequent advanced study in this classical art have given me the foundation I still rely on today. Those classes also made me aware that icing and finishing a cake with good pipework remain vital skills in the cake-decorating industry.

Those early piping classes provided the framework and discipline needed to pursue the various international techniques I wanted to learn. Australian-style cake decorating or variations on this style have become my trademark. The precision piping, strenuous control, and discipline that this style demands has given me the structure I have always longed for in an art form. I was also attracted to English and South African sugar art because these intricate styles are just as demanding and precise.

Besides in the United States, Canada, Australia, New Zealand, South Africa, the British Isles, and European countries, the art of cake decorating exists in many other countries, notably the Caribbean Islands, the Philippines, Argentina, Mexico, Brazil, and many more. Each nation's style is unique and unbelievably beautiful. What links these many styles as well as what makes them different is their color, strong design concepts, precision, and pipework.

In America today we're seeing less and less piping on cakes. All-occasion cakes found at corner bakeries often have more piping than custom cakes created for black-tie gatherings and special events, served as the final course in haute-cuisine restaurants, or shown in the pages of fashionable magazines. This upscale trend of favoring cakes with rolled icing and little or no piping has become more popular at weddings and formal events. Many cake designers no longer feel compelled to pull out that pastry bag to add finishing touches to the cake.

(*opposite page*) Crystal Wedding Cake, designed by Toba Garrett. The photo by Wendell T. Webber originally appeared in *In Style Weddings*, spring 2002.

I'm just the opposite. I find it hard not to pipe something, although I'm asked from time to time to produce cakes without piping. For me, personally, a cake without some form of pipework seems incomplete.

If you've tried your hand at cake decorating, you know that the breathtaking cake found at the center of a lavish gathering involves not simply time and an aesthetic sensibility, but mastery of many skills and techniques.

For elegant cake design, piping is one of the most important skills a decorator can possess. The abilities to ice the cake smoothly, cover it beautifully in rolled icing, and produce realistic piped and hand-shaped flowers are also important. Flower arranging, choosing just the right colors and color combinations, as well as being able to create them in chosen icings are essential to the art. You'll also want to focus on composition, balance, and the execution of appropriate themes. Most cake-decorating skills can be learned; however, pulling them all together in a design that wins every guest's admiration comes with practice. Of course, it's helpful to have not just a steady hand but a good eye and sense of design. After all, cake design aspires to high art; edible art in most cases, but art just the same.

We've organized this book into chapters to give you a master class in cake decorating, beginning with specific skill-building tech-niques, such as splitting, filling, and icing a cake, and ending with intricately piped and hand-sculpted designs. We hope to provide both beginners and advanced students insights into the beauty and depth of the art. We also hope that seasoned cake decorators will find this book a good resource to review techniques and pick up new ones. Students new to the art can also draw on these pages to learn profes-sional techniques and perfect skills at their own pace.

We've included Master Chef's Hints so that you'll know some professional secrets to make your cakes just that much better. We've also created a few helpful charts so that you can puzzle out certain icing mysteries, such as how to achieve just the right color that even sometimes eludes the pros.

Whatever your experience and talents, we hope to encourage you to pull out your mixer, pick up a pastry bag or modeling paste, and begin to enjoy the art that keeps me smiling.

—*Toba Garrett*

CHAPTER 1

Cake-Decorating Tools

Seasoned cake designers collect supplies and equipment that aid them in creating cakes from the simplest to the most elegant works of art. If you're like me, you can never have too many decorating tools and kitchen gadgets. Invest in good-quality equipment and tools from the very beginning; they'll have an enduring effect on your cakes. With them you can work confidently and with greater ease.

Cake-decorating stores will have most of the tools shown in the photos on these pages. A few tools and ingredients are available only through specialty suppliers (see Special Cake-Decorating Supplies on pp. 170–171).

In later chapters, when demonstrating particular techniques, we'll introduce more supplies, such as icing bars, cake smoothers, and a few other helpful tools.

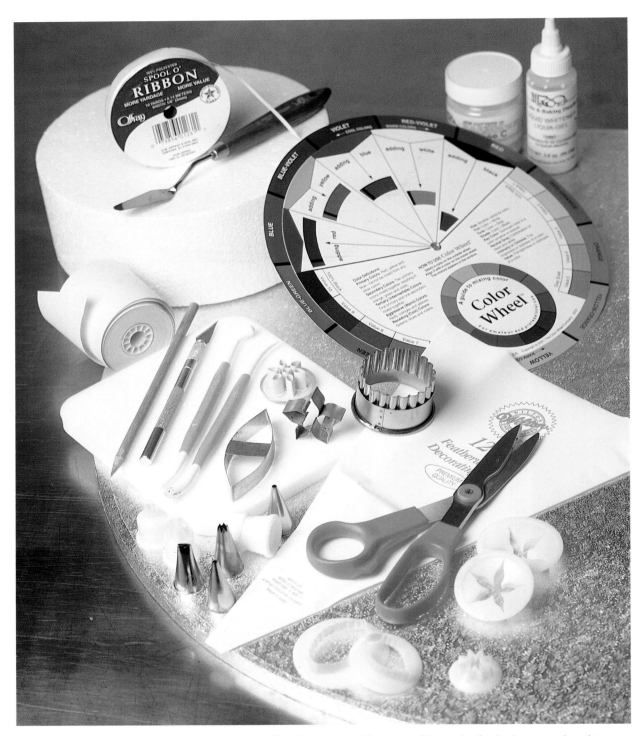

Beginning at 9 o'clock and sitting on a white cell pad are a modeling stick, X-acto knife, dogbone tool, quilting wheel, assorted metal cutters, and English embroidery cutter (embroidery anglaise). Reading counterclockwise are an assortment of metal piping tips with couplers, pastry bag, kitchen scissors, assortment of plastic gumpaste cutters, color wheel, liquid whitener (white food color), Tylose C, Styrofoam, palette knife, satin ribbon, and adding-machine tape. Everything rests on a silver board that can be used for cake presentation.

BASICS

good mixer (with attachments)
mixing bowls
baking pans (all sizes and shapes)
rolling pins
rubber and wooden spatulas
turntable (professional)
liquid and dry measuring cups
measuring spoons
cake foils
pastry brushes
cardboard cake boards
offset metal spatulas
kitchen scissors

SPECIAL TOOLS

paste, gel, and powdered food
  colors
nonstick rolling pins
silver and gold powders
leaf presses
plastic smoothers
crimper selections
assorted brushes (sable, Chinese)
textured rolling pins
plastic stamens
fine, covered florist's wires
cameo and other wooden molds
gumpaste flower cutters
assortment of piping tips
impression stamps
X-acto knives

ball tools
veining tools
satin ribbons
palette knife
color wheel
gum tragacanth, Tylose, and gum
  Arabic
Styrofoam dummies
adding-machine paper
surface grip
kitchen scissors
florist's tape
embroidery scissors
candy thermometer
quilting wheel
icing nail

This icing nail, used the other way up, helps shape flowers in their various petal stages.

Counterclockwise from 9 o'clock are Chinese, all-purpose, and sable paintbrushes; an assortment of crimpers; white plastic smoothers; leaf press; gold and silver dusting powder; assortment of petal dust; gel food colors (in bottles); nonstick rolling pin; lace press; fine, covered florist's wires; plastic cameo mold, two wooden presses; and plastic stamens. The tools rest on a surface grip, silver cake board, and small white acrylic board.

CHAPTER 2

The Icings
That Make the Cake

Whether you're a busy professional cake designer or a weekend hobbyist, you can never have too many icings on hand. Icings are usually classified as creamy or rolled. Creamy icings may be smoothed over the cake or used to pipe borders and flowers. Rolled icings may cover the cake with a beautifully smooth surface or be used to hand-sculpt flowers, fashion plaques, or create small three-dimensional sculptures.

Ultimately, you may consider one or two to be your best icings and the others as second or third best. Actually, the cake project will determine what icing to use or what combination of icings to use. We often use creamy and rolled

icings together to achieve a certain look. Cakes with rolled icing are more expensive because they generally require a lot of detailing, such as pipework and hand-shaped flowers.

Sometimes I use my second or third choice of icing as a filling between cake layers instead of using a preserve or freshly made filling. I also use them at home when entertaining informally.

You'll find recipes for all these various icings, buttercreams, meringues, rolled fondants, and royal icing, as well as for modeling chocolate, ganache, marzipan, gumpaste, pastillage, sieved apricot jam, lemon curd, Isomalt sugar, gilding, spackled paste, and more in Chapter 10.

Creamy Icings

Several icings are in this category. Choose the creamy icing that performs best for you, or, the occasion or environment may dictate which icing is preferred. Remember, you may or may not like an icing because, for instance, you consider it too sweet or sugary; however, the person for whom you are preparing the cake may love that particular icing. Consider classifying your icings into occasions, i.e., birthdays, weddings, children's parties, home entertaining, and other occasions. That way, you will know which icing to refer to when that occasion comes up.

DECORATOR'S BUTTERCREAM Usually this is the first icing that comes to mind. It is sweet and has a familiar smell and taste. It is largely made with confectioners' sugar, butter, vegetable shortening, liquids, and salt. Decorator's buttercream is also easy to make and doesn't require a lot of preparation time. I have used this icing on birthday cakes for adults or for children. I often use this for a child's birthday cake.

SWISS MERINGUE BUTTERCREAM This is a more sophisticated icing with a great deal of butter. Swiss meringue buttercream is also a cooked icing. (In a double boiler, you whisk the egg whites and sugar over a pot of simmering water.) It has a grown-up taste; that's because a lot of alcohol or liqueur is generally used to cut back the buttery flavor. This is definitely an adult birthday-cake or wedding-cake icing.

MASTER CHEF'S HINT

Use Swiss meringue buttercream as a base icing and convert it to white chocolate, amaretto mocha, or amaretto praline mocha buttercream.

Icings (from left to right): Swiss meringue buttercream, decorator's buttercream, French vanilla buttercream, chocolate buttercream, and royal icing. The round metal piping tips are #2 and #3.

CHOCOLATE BUTTERCREAM ICING We all know a few people who do not like or cannot eat chocolate. This is truly a shame because this is one of my favorite icings. Needless to say, it's appropriate for almost any occasion. This buttercream version takes a lot of preparation, but it's worth every minute. The secret of this chocolate buttercream icing is the incorporation of refrigerated ganache that gives it a sinful taste. Sometimes I use praline instead of ganache for a delicious change. Chocolate buttercream icing can be for a birthday cake or groom's cake icing.

ROYAL ICING In America royal icing, although creamy, is considered more of an ornamental icing. Outside the United States, most decorated cakes are iced in royal icing. These are rich fruitcakes which first have a layer of marzipan.

This icing is made in two ways, with egg white or with meringue powder. In the United States, we don't generally use royal icing on cakes because it dries quickly and hard and is not usually flavorful. In the Caribbean Islands, my colleagues and decorating friends use vanilla extract and rum to flavor their royal icings. You can arrest the hard drying by stirring a little glycerine into the icing after it has been beaten. The glycerine will allow the icing to dry on the outside yet remain soft on the inside.

We do, however, use royal icing as a finishing icing on a cake that has been covered with marzipan or rolled fondant. It gives the cake a classically finished look.

In the United States, this icing is often used to decorate cookies or glue gingerbread houses together. Royal icing is an icing for more formal events, such as weddings or anniversaries.

FRENCH VANILLA BUTTERCREAM This icing actually tastes like vanilla ice cream. The milk and sugar are heated together, which dissolves the granulated sugar. Butter, all-purpose flour (yes, flour), vanilla, and a pinch of salt make this icing remarkable. For a richer taste, substitute heavy cream for the milk.

The only drawback is that French Vanilla Buttercream isn't as stable for the outside coating of the cake as other icings. Applying two or three coats of this icing can arrest the problem. This is an icing you'll want to use at home for informal gatherings or family occasions. I prefer to use this icing as a delicious filling or for birthday cakes.

Rolled Icings

Rolled icings, usually reserved for special occasions, are formal-looking. Several icings are in this category. Perhaps the best known is rolled fondant (what we call it in America). Chocolate rolled fondant, as well as white and dark modeling chocolates, are better tasting than white rolled fondant. Marzipan may be used to cover cakes and is far better tasting than rolled fondant. As with creamy icings, the event will dictate what rolled icing to use or perhaps what combination of icings to use.

This fruitcake was first iced in marzipan, then in royal icing. The piped flowers are in royal icing.

WHITE AND CHOCOLATE ROLLED FONDANT

White and chocolate rolled fondant are staples for busy cake designers. Rolled fondants are also called sugarpaste, which is exactly what they are. These icings are confectioners' sugar-based and have corn syrup, flavoring, gelatin (in homemade paste), vanilla, gum products (for strength and stretch), and a few other ingredients. They're first rolled out like pie dough and then rolled over a cake that has been first thinly coated with buttercream. Not all people enjoy eating this type of icing, although they love the way it looks. You can flavor white or chocolate rolled fondant with extracts, alcohols, liqueurs, and candy oils.

Buy rolled fondant at cake-decorating stores under commercial names like Pettinice, Regalice, Satin Ice, and Wilton Rolled Fondant. These work nicely, but you can make rolled fondant from scratch.

CHOCOLATE ROLLED FONDANT For chocolate rolled fondant, simply add cocoa powder to white rolled fondant and perhaps a little chocolate liqueur (like Godiva). The flavor is delicious. You can also buy commercial chocolate rolled fondant.

These rolled icings are (top to bottom) chocolate rolled fondant, white rolled fondant, marzipan, gumpaste, white modeling chocolate, and pastillage.

This cake is iced in chocolate rolled fondant. The raspberries were made with marzipan.

MODELING CHOCOLATES Several types of chocolates fall into this category; basics are dark, white, and milk. Modeling chocolates are delicious alternatives to rolled fondants. However, these chocolates are rarely used to cover cakes. Modeling chocolates are usually reserved for hand-shaped flowers, leaves, and ribbons that adorn cakes. They can, however, drape cakes. That's because modeling chocolates, especially white and milk, contain a large amount of butterfat that makes them flexible enough to be rolled out to cover the chosen cake. Dark modeling chocolate will dry too quickly to be used for traditional icings. You can, however, roll strips of dark modeling chocolate to cover the cake's sides. Then, you can roll out a large circle and cut a circular disk to cover the cake's top.

MARZIPAN Marzipan is another delicious alternative to rolled fondant. However, it is not as flexible as rolled fondant. Marzipan is made of almond paste, confectioners' sugar, corn syrup, and flavoring. If you make marzipan the conventional way it is created in the United States, its color will be beige. Adding rolled fondant to the marzipan will create a lighter color and creamier taste. (See recipe on p. 140.)

Marzipan is rarely used as an outer covering for cakes. We find it not refined, flexible, or smooth enough. In England, Australia, South Africa, and some other countries, marzipan is popularly used as an undercoat icing. Then the cake is iced with royal icing or rolled fondant, which creates a thick coating of icing when the cake is cut. With this technique, the cake can be preserved for some time.

In America, marzipan is largely used to make hand-shaped fruits, vegetables, and animals for a lovely centerpiece or as decoration on a cake.

These tiny fruit shapes were created with marzipan. Petal dust adds a little natural color. A clove sliver makes a tiny stem.

GUMPASTE Gumpaste is an ornamental icing, chiefly used to create lifelike flowers to adorn a cake. Gumpaste is not eaten because it's not palatable. It can also be used to make free-standing ornaments that adorn a cake or act as a centerpiece.

This gumpaste flower bouquet uses florist's stem wires and cotton-thread stamens.

Apart from traditional recipes, you can make a quick gumpaste by simply adding gum tragacanth or Tylose to white rolled fondant, or buy ready-made gumpaste.

PASTILLAGE Pastillage is another ornamental icing for making plaques and three-dimensional sculptures.

A variety of recipes work. With pastillage you can create greeting cards, placecards, and three-dimensional buildings or other structures that you want to last. Objects made of pastillage are always centerpieces that are not eaten because they can remain perfect showpieces lasting for years.

These heart-shaped boxes created from pastillage will last for months and even years.

LAVENDER 1 oz White + ⅛ toothpick Soft Pink + ⅛ toothpick Violet

BABY BLUE 1 oz White + ¼ toothpick Sky Blue + ⅛ toothpick Violet

TEAL 1 oz White + ¼ toothpick Lemon Yellow + ¼ toothpick Sky Blue

MOSS GREEN 1 oz White + ¼ toothpick Leaf Green + ⅛ toothpick Chocolate Brown

AMERICAN PEACH 1 oz White + ¹⁄₁₆ toothpick Lemon Yellow + ¹⁄₁₆ toothpick Soft Pink + ¹⁄₁₆ toothpick Orange

CHARTREUSE 1 oz White + ¼ toothpick Lemon Yellow + ¼ toothpick Leaf Green

RED 1 oz White + 1 toothpick Egg Yellow + ¼ toothpick Violet + ¹⁄₁₆ tsp Christmas Red + ¹⁄₁₆ tsp Super Red

IVORY 1 oz White + ⅛ toothpick Deep Pink + ⅛ toothpick Lemon Yellow + ⅛ toothpick Chocolate Brown

BLACK 1 oz White + 1 toothpick Leaf Green + 1 toothpick Chocolate Brown and Violet + ⅛ tsp Super Black

Color Techniques

Often when teaching classes, I find students complaining that they cannot obtain certain types of colors, especially reds and blacks. Only through teaching, experimenting, and learning from my students have I developed a series of techniques to achieve a particular shade.

The colors in Toba's Color Chart use 1 ounce (28 g) of royal icing mixed with various gel food colors added on a toothpick. The toothpick measure, whether ¹⁄₁₆, ⅛, or ¼, indicates how deeply you dip the toothpick into the given food color gel before transferring it to the bowl of icing you're preparing. The color names, like Leaf Green or Chocolate Brown, are those given on common commercial brands. Please remember that these colors and amounts are approximate; you'll need to experiment with different amounts of color to obtain true shades.

CHAPTER 3

Preparing & Icing the Cake

Few skills are more important to the success of finished cakes than the proper execution of splitting and filling the cake and applying smooth icing before you begin to decorate. The more care you take in these procedures, the better the results in a balanced, structured, and sturdy cake. Your decoration skills may be superb, but if the cake looks like the leaning tower of Pisa, you're in trouble.

No specific number of layers are required for putting a cake together; however, the more layers, the higher the cake. Generally, two to perhaps five very thin layers can appear attractive and appetizing and be well-structured when plated. Remember, the inside appearance of the cake is just as important as its outside. Even layers with appropriate filling can look most delicious and demonstrate a high level of professionalism.

These steps for splitting and filling the cake, icing it and smoothing the icing, spackling the cake with icing and cake scraps, covering the cake with rolled fondant, and tiering the cake will help you achieve that perfect finish.

Splitting & Filling

First, we'll level the top of the cake so that it is as flat as possible. Then we'll split and level the cake layers. I often prefer using a single baking pan that's 3 or 4 inches (7.6 to 10 cm) deep. Then, I split the cake into three layers (with each layer 1 to 1½ inches or 2.5 to 3.8 cm high).

SPLITTING THE CAKE To split the cake, first place the cake on a turntable or a cardboard circle or square. (Buy these corrugated cardboard circles or squares at cake-decorating stores.) Position the serrated knife on the cake at 3 o'clock on the clock dial, if you're right-handed. Position your opposite hand on the cake. Move the serrated knife blade so that it faces the side of the cake at one-third the distance from the top of the cake. Turn the cake counterclockwise as you score the cake and move the knife clockwise. (Reverse procedures if you're left-handed.) After you go completely around, apply a sawing motion to the scored line and sever the first one-third of the cake. Slide a cardboard circle or square under the cake layer to prevent it from breaking.

LEVELING THE CAKE LAYERS Repeat this procedure for the second and third layers of the cake. After each layer is on a separate cardboard, level each layer separately if it doesn't look even. Now you'll have three even layers even if you didn't split them evenly to begin with. Put the cake slivers aside; we'll use them later.

THE FINAL CARDBOARD Second, put a little buttercream icing in the center of the final cardboard. Slide the first layer into the center of the finished cardboard. Remember: use the cardboard to transfer the first layer to the finished board. Use the cardboard to press on the cake to adhere it to the buttercream icing on the cardboard.

DAMMING THE CAKE Next pipe a layer of buttercream icing using a #18 star tip around the circumference on top of the individual cake layer. This is called damming the cake. The dam

DAMMING THE CAKE

To create a dam for the filling, pipe icing around the cake's circumference, using a #18 star piping tip.

We've added lemon curd filling, carefully pouring it into the center of the cake, then smoothing it out in all directions inside the icing dam around the top of the cake's perimeter. It's best to keep the filling layer thin, and smooth the filling until it just reaches the dam. Too much filling may cause the top cake layer to slide off.

protects the filling from oozing out of the cake. The line should be just inside the edge of the cake layer. (See photos on p. 21.) If your filling is buttercream, a light mousse, or a light layer of cream filling, then this dam may not be necessary.

(See photos on p. 21.)

MASTER CHEF'S HINT

Before filling the cake, pipe a thin layer of icing inside the circumference of the top of the cake to prevent the filling from oozing out. This will help create a finished look.

A thin layer of filling often works best. A thick layer could cause the layer(s) to slide off.

FILLING THE CAKE Carefully pour or spoon a thin layer of filling inside the piped dam line. If the filling is too thick, the layers could slide apart.

ADDING THE SECOND LAYER Position the next layer over the first layer, using the cardboard to transfer the second layer on top of the first. Use the cardboard to press lightly on the second layer. Repeat the procedure of piping a layer of buttercream icing around the circumference of the cake, followed by the filling.

CRUMB COATING Secure the last layer on top of the second. Smooth a thin layer of buttercream icing over the sides and top of the cake (to secure the crumbs). This is called crumb coating.

MASTER CHEF'S HINT

Crumb coating secures the crumbs on the cake with a thin layer of buttercream. This undercoat icing won't be visible on the finished cake even when it's cut and served. This technique prevents crumbs from getting into the finished icing.

Use a cake cardboard to transfer the second layer on top of the first layer.

CRUMB COATING

To crumb coat the cake, use a long, offset metal spatula to add a thin layer of buttercream icing to the cake. This will prevent cake crumbs from being picked up by the finished icing.

The large photo (right) shows a cake that has been completely crumb coated. First it was leveled, then split, dammed, and filled. Then the second layer was added, dammed, and filled again, and the third layer added.

Begin with a crumb-coated cake. Pipe buttercream icing, using a #18 star tip in a pastry bag loaded with icing, on the sides of the cake, piping on the sides from bottom to top to bottom. Pipe back and forth across the top of the cake.

SMOOTHING THE ICING

Dip an offset metal spatula in hot water, then dry it. Using the metal spatula, smooth the icing on the cake, beginning with the side and removing any excess to create a smooth finish.

Piped Buttercream Icing

PIPED TECHNIQUE FOR APPLYING ICING

Fill a large pastry bag with buttercream icing and a #18 star tip. Starting at 6 o'clock on the clock dial, pipe lines of icing up and down from the top to the bottom of the cake.

This provides more than enough icing on the cake. Pipe lines back and forth on the top of the cake.

MASTER CHEF'S HINT

If you're right-handed, you'll want to pipe counterclockwise while turning the cake clockwise. If you're left-handed, you'll want to pipe clockwise, while turning the cake counterclockwise. Thus, a right-handed person starts at 9 o'clock and a left-handed person at 3 o'clock.

SMOOTHING THE ICING

With an offset metal spatula dipped in hot water and dried, position the spatula at 9 o'clock at a 45° angle against the cake. Move the spatula counterclockwise as you turn the cake clockwise. Be careful not to take too much icing off the cake.

Pre-ice the cake's sides in one turn. This allows the icing on the sides to rise up higher than the piped icing on the cake's top. Then, position the offset spatula at 6 o'clock on the clock dial at a 45° angle. Move the spatula from 6 o'clock toward 12 o'clock, ending before you reach the other side. Turn the cake clockwise as you continue to do this.

To finish the look, position a hot and dry spatula flat against the cake at 9 o'clock. Apply light pressure as you turn the cake clockwise. Position the spatula at 6 o'clock at a 45° angle and move across the cake to finish the top of the cake. Turn the cake slowly as you create a clean, crisp edge.

Ultimately, you want an illusion of smoothness. Remember, you are going to pipe top and bottom borders. Thus, the cake doesn't need to look absolutely perfect. Sometimes, the more care you put into making the cake perfect, the more imperfect it becomes.

Spackling the Cake

This new technique, devised in my kitchen, gives the cake more stability, structure, and a professional look, especially when the cake has been covered in rolled fondant. Spackled paste is actually cake crumbs, icing, and filling combined in a thick paste. Spackling should be done before icing the cake.

Rolled iced cakes in America sometimes seem to sag in the middle and cake layers are often visible through rolled fondant. This presents an unbalanced and unprofessional-looking cake. Perhaps the crumb coating was not thick enough, or, the cake wasn't leveled evenly, or the cake was not refrigerated long enough, thereby allowing the crumb coat to set.

I developed the spackling technique when trying to achieve the look of Australian- or English-style cakes without adding more icing or marzipan. In England, Australia, or South Africa, fruitcakes are used for many celebrations. Fruitcakes are patched with marzipan to fill in any holes or crevices. The cake is then three-fourths or completely covered in marzipan, which gives

Apply spackled paste over the cake crumb coated with buttercream, turning the cake plate as you go. Begin with the sides and finish with the top. The spackled paste will fill in any uneven spots on the cake's surface so that your finished icing, whether a rolled fondant or a buttercream, will appear smooth and professional. Spackled paste is a mixture of cake crumbs, icing, and filling.

SMOOTHING THE SPACKLED PASTE

Smooth the spackled paste with an offset metal spatula. The far right photo shows the finished spackled cake. Refrigerate the cake to allow the spackled paste to set. You can then coat the spackling with a thin layer of buttercream to help the rolled fondant adhere.

the cake stability and structure. The marzipan and other icing layers also help preserve the fruitcake. Then the fruitcake receives a layer of rolled fondant or royal icing. As a result, the fruitcake will have at least a ½ inch (1.3 cm) thick cake icing that gives the cake a perfect finish for decorating.

Since fruitcakes are not often eaten in the America, we need to structure our yellow, chocolate, or pound cakes in such a way that we achieve that perfectly smooth finish seen in the British Commonwealth.

MASTER CHEF'S HINT

Use spackled paste as a filling between layers. People will swear that it's a lovely nutty filling.

Last, the spackled paste is great to use if you damage the cake or parts of its sides or top. Spackled paste can help rebuild the cake.

Break up the cake by hand. (Here is where those cake crumbs from leveling the cake come in handy.) Then, add some buttercream icing to help glue the fondant to the spackled paste. Add some cake filling to sandwich everything together. Stir with a wooden spoon or rubber spatula to make a thick paste.

Next apply a layer of spackled paste about ⅛ to ¼ inch (3 to 6 mm) thick to the cake, starting on its sides. Use warm water or additional buttercream next to the spackled paste to help smooth it. Then ice the top of the cake with spackled paste.

TO FIND THE CAKE'S MEASUREMENTS

Measure the cake's diameter (width or length, measured across the top) + height on left side + height on right side + 1 or 2 extra inches (2.5 to 5 cm) for good measure.

Total = Cake's Measurements
Diameter of rolled fondant needed.

After it has been spackled, refrigerate the cake until firm. Loosely cover the spackled cake with plastic wrap and let the cake sit overnight or at least several hours in the refrigerator. Then cover the spackled cake with a thin layer of buttercream icing to help the rolled fondant to stick to the cake.

Covering the Cake with Rolled Fondant

First, the cake should be spackled or lightly iced with a buttercream icing. Refrigerate the cake overnight if possible, or let it rest in the refrigerator for 2 to 4 hours or until firm.

Remove the cake from the refrigerator and lightly ice with buttercream. This thin new coating of buttercream icing will allow the rolled icing to stick to the cake. If you choose,

COATING THE SPACKLED CAKE WITH BUTTERCREAM

Apply a thin new layer of buttercream icing to the spackled cake before you ice it with rolled fondant. This will ensure that the fondant adheres to the cake.

Dust the surface with cornstarch or a mixture of confectioners' sugar and cornstarch. Use a rolling pin to roll out the fondant into a circle. Turn the fondant in one-eighth increments as you apply light pressure. Finally, when you're ready, roll the fondant onto the rolling pin to lift and transfer the rolled icing to the cake.

COVERING THE CAKE WITH ROLLED FONDANT

In one motion, unroll the fondant from the rolling pin onto the cake. The thin layer of buttercream will help the fondant adhere to the cake.

you can mist the cake with water instead of using additional buttercream.

Roll the rolled icing out ¼ inch (6 mm) thick (circular if a round cake or rectangular if a square cake). To calculate the cake's measurements, consult the chart Calculating Rolled Fondant Sizes on p. 29, or use the formula To Find the Cake's Measurements on p. 27.

Second, dust the surface with cornstarch or a mixture of cornstarch and confectioners' sugar. Shape the fondant into a round disk (about 6 inches or 15 cm in diameter). Roll out the fondant, working quickly because the fondant will begin to dry. If you add a little glycerine to homemade fondant it will remain a little softer to give you a longer time to work. You can also add a little vegetable shortening to commercial rolled fondant to make it more flexible.

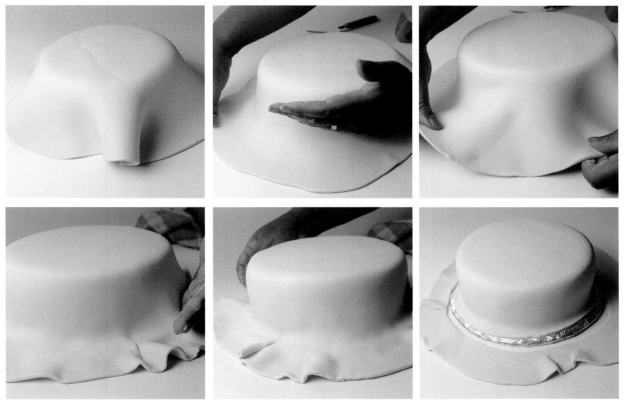

With light pressure, gently adjust the fondant so that it adheres to the cake. Then cut away excess fondant with an X-acto knife or metal spatula around the cake cardboard (ours was covered with gold foil).

CALCULATING ROLLED FONDANT SIZES

Cake's Diameter	Height of Cake's Sides	Rolled Fondant Diameter Desired
6 inches (15 cm)	3 inches (7.5 cm) x 2	13 to 14 inches (33 to 35 cm)
6 inches (15 cm)	4 inches (10 cm) x 2	15 to 16 inches (38 to 40 cm)
8 inches (20 cm)	3 inches (7.5 cm) x 2	15 to 16 inches (38 to 40 cm)
8 inches (20 cm)	4 inches (10 cm) x 2	17 to 18 inches (43 to 45 cm)
10 inches (25 cm)	3 inches (7.5 cm) x 2	17 to 18 inches (43 to 45 cm)
10 inches (25 cm)	4 inches (10 cm) x 2	19 to 20 inches (48 to 50 cm)
12 inches (30 cm)	3 inches (7.5 cm) x 2	19 to 20 inches (48 to 50 cm)
12 inches (30 cm)	4 inches (10 cm) x 2	21 to 22 inches (53 to 56 cm)
14 inches (35 cm)	3 inches (7.5 cm) x 2	21 to 22 inches (53 to 56 cm)
14 inches (35 cm)	4 inches (10 cm) x 2	23 to 24 inches (58 to 61 cm)
16 inches (40 cm)	3 inches (7.5 cm) x 2	23 to 24 inches (58 to 61 cm)
16 inches (40 cm)	4 inches (10 cm) x 2	25 to 26 inches (63 to 66 cm)

Note: Metric measurements are rounded off.

After you've adjusted the fit, push the rolled fondant to the edge of the cake. Then use the edge of an offset metal spatula to cut away the excess rolled fondant. Then seal the bottom edge of the fondant to the cake to prevent air from getting to the cake.

SMOOTHING THE ROLLED FONDANT ON THE CAKE

Use cake smoothers, pressing lightly, to smooth the fondant on the cake.

When rolling the fondant into a circle, turn the fondant in one-eighth increments as you apply light to heavy pressure. For a rectangular shape, turn the fondant in one-quarter increments. Roll the fondant, starting at 12 o'clock on the clockface, onto a rolling pin, brushing away excess cornstarch as you roll it.

Third, start at the cake board at 6 o'clock on the clockface and quickly roll the fondant over the cake. Very lightly roll the rolling pin over the fondant to squash any air pockets. Lift up any folds with one hand and use the other hand to lightly brush and smooth it out as you adhere the fondant to the cake. Never try to force a fold to adhere to a cake. Continue to lift up folds and smooth out the fondant on the cake. Then take both hands (not fingers) and apply light pressure around the base of the cake.

MASTER CHEF'S HINT

Instead of using a rolling pin, when you're ready to transfer the rolled fondant to the cake, simply roll up your sleeves, tuck your hands and arms under the fondant, and place it over the cake.

Fourth, cut away the excess, leaving ½ inch (1.3 cm) near the bottom of the cake. Now, hold an offset spatula at a 45° angle at 6 o'clock on the clockface. Starting at the rolled fondant's edge, push the fondant to the cake's edge and apply pressure to cut away excess fondant. Turn the cake in one-eighth increments and continue with the same technique.

After you go around the cake, check to see that no excess fondant is extending from the cake. Now, hold the offset spatula at a 45° angle with a firm grip. Push the spatula against the cake, and turn the cake and the spatula to seal off the cake and leave a perfect finish. If you push the fondant to the edge of the cake, you won't cut the fondant too short, which would allow air to get to the cake.

Fifth, completely smooth the cake using two white plastic cake smoothers. Apply pressure as you go around the cake to adhere the fondant to the cake and complete the structuring. Smooth the top.

After you've finished smoothing the top, you're ready to tier the cake.

Tiering the Cake

To build cake tiers, first, determine whether the tier above the bottom will be centered or off-center. Measure the area of the bottom tier using a cardboard cake circle or square. The circle or square should be the exact size of the cake you are putting on top. Using a toothpick, pinprick tiny holes around the cardboard. Remove the cardboard. Use these holes as a guide for positioning the second cake layer. This is called the pattern.

MAKING A PATTERN TO POSITION THE SECOND TIER

The cake iced with rolled fondant (left) will become the first tier of the finished cake. The chef is using a standard cake cardboard circle that's the exact size of the second tier. Around the cardboard, she pinpricks holes into the cake below (the base tier) to create a pattern to guide her in positioning the second tier.

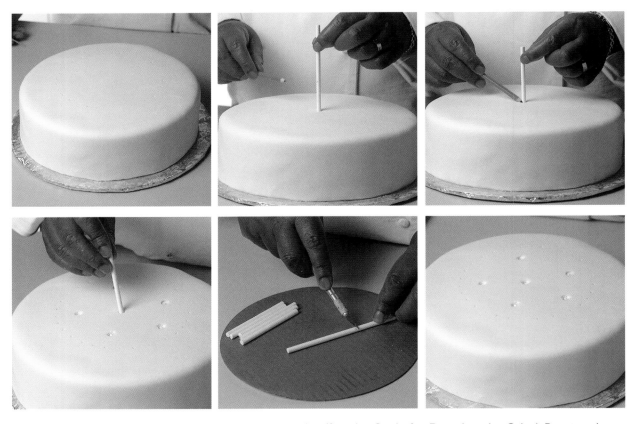

Determine how many dowels you will need for the cake. (See the Guide for Doweling the Cake.) Position the first dowel in the center of the pattern you created. Push the dowel into the cake until it touches the cardboard below, and mark the dowel's height with a pencil. Remove the dowel and cut it ⅛ inch (3 mm) lower than the pencil mark. Replace the dowel. Position other dowels equally around the center dowel and about ½ to ¾ inch (1.3 to 1.9 cm) inside the perimeter of your pattern noting the position of the second layer.

TOBA'S GUIDE FOR DOWELING THE CAKE

CAKE DIAMETER	DOWELS NEEDED
4 inches or 10 cm	3 to 4
6 inches or 15 cm	5 to 6
8 inches or 20 cm	7
9 inches or 23 cm	8
10 inches or 25 cm	9
12 inches or 30 cm	11
14 inches or 35 cm	13
16 inches or 40 cm	15
18 inches or 45 cm	17
20 inches or 50 cm	19

Next dowel the cake using lollipop sticks, straws, wooden dowels, etc. I use lollypop sticks because they are safe and strong and can be cut with a pair of scissors or scored with an X-acto knife and snipped off. See the Guide for Doweling the Cake to determine the number of dowels needed.

Position the first dowel in the center of the pattern. Push the dowel down until it touches the cardboard attached to the cake. Use a pencil to mark the point where the cake and dowel ends. Remove the dowel and cut the dowel ⅛ inch (3 mm) lower than the pencil mark. Replace the dowel in the cake.

If you cut the dowel lower than the pencil mark, the top tier will sink slightly to the dowel and reduce the negative space between the top and bottom tiers. Little to no space will remain between the tiers and less correction will be necessary.

Next position the other dowels equally around the center dowel. Begin at the pattern's perimeter (outer edge) and move each dowel ½ to ¾ inch (1.3 to 1.9 cm) inside the pattern. Mark, cut, and replace the dowels.

Last, put a small amount of icing inside the pattern. The icing should extend from the pattern's center up to ½ inch (1.3 cm) from the pattern's perimeter. Carefully place the top tier on the bottom tier, using the pattern as a guide. Use a long, wide metal spatula and your hands to place one tier on top of another.

Example: How many dowels are needed to tier a cake with 14-inch, 10-inch, and 6-inch layers? Since the 10-inch layer is sitting on the 14-inch layer, you'll need support dowels for a 10-inch. Because the 6-inch layer is sitting on the 10-inch, you'll need the support dowel for a 6-inch. Thus, you'll need 9 dowels for the 10-inch and 5 to 6 dowels for the 6-inch.

Finally, after you have inserted all the dowels, cover the dowels and dowel holes with a thin layer of icing. This will also help seal the second tier over the first.

TIERING THE CAKE

Carefully position the second tier over the pattern and its circle of icing in the base tier. Use a long, wide, offset metal spatula and then both hands to position the second tier exactly. The icing below will help seal the new layer.

Royal Iced Cakes

The technique for applying royal icing isn't widely used in the United States. In America royal icing is used as a decorative icing that usually isn't eaten. However, in the Caribbean Islands, England, South Africa, Australia, the Philippines, and many other countries, royal icing is often used to ice cakes and commonly eaten.

Often a rich fruitcake first completely covered in marzipan gains three or more coats of royal icing to finish it. To Americanize this technique, we've used a firm pound cake for demonstration.

First, make a recipe of Marzipan and Meringue Powder Royal Icing. (See chapter 10 pp. 138 and 140.) Cut and trim the cake. Fill any holes in the cake with little pieces of marzipan. Use a metal offset spatula to seal it to the cake. Next dust the work surface with a little powered sugar. Roll out on confectioners' sugar some marzipan paste so that it's about ¼ inch (6 mm) thick. Roll the paste out so that it is larger than the cake's circumference. Brush the center of the marzipan with sieved apricot jam. Carefully lift the cake and place it on the marzipan with sieved jam. Press on top of the cake to seal it to the marzipan.

Trim the excess marzipan from around the cake base. The excess paste can be rerolled and reused. Place a small amount of royal icing in the center of the finished cake board. Carefully pick up the cake and flip it over. The marzipan bottom is now on top. Place the bottom of the cake on the iced board. Press lightly to secure the cake to the board. Brush the sides of the cake with sieved apricot jam or a little buttercream.

Measure the height and diameter of the cake. Roll out a long strip of marzipan ¼ inch (6 mm) thick. Cut and trim the paste to the size of the cake. Carefully pick up the paste and attach it to the cake's sides. Cut away any excess. The cake is now ready to be iced in royal icing.

Roughly spread royal icing on the sides of the marzipan-iced cake. Make sure that you get icing from the top of the cake to the bottom of the cake. Smooth lightly with an offset spatula. Next place a small round cardboard on the top of the marzipan cake. This prevents damage from fingerprint marks to the marzipan on top. Place your opposite hand on the cardboard and turn the cake clockwise as far as you can without removing your hands. Now take a side scraper (or bench scraper) and position it at 12 o'clock on the clock dial. The side scraper

Brush with sieved apricot jam the center of the rolled-out marzipan. Place the cake on the marzipan and sieved jam, press the top of the cake to seal it to the marzipan, and cut around the circumference of the cake. Remove excess marzipan.

Cover the sides of the cake with a strip of marzipan cut to the height of the sides. Then ice with royal icing. Use a cake scraper to remove excess royal icing. To hold the cake firmly and prevent fingerprints in the marzipan, use a cake cardboard.

After two or three more coats of royal icing, the marzipan, once visible through the icing, will disappear. Lightly smooth the icing with an offset metal spatula. Then take a long cake smoother and pull it toward you over the top of the cake with your hands close together.

Use an offset metal spatula to remove excess icing from the sides. Then use a metal spatula to smooth the cake's sides. Finally, ice and smooth the cake board.

should be positioned at a 45° angle. Next turn the cake counterclockwise as you move your hands clockwise, icing the cake in one turn. Use an offset spatula to clean up the top edge of the cake. This is the first icing layer and you will still see a lot of the marzipan through the royal icing. After two to three more coats, the marzipan will disappear. Let dry for 4 to 6 hours.

Next roughly spread icing on the top of the cake. Lightly smooth it with an offset spatula. Take a long cake smoother (or a very long spatula) and hold it at a 45° angle at 12 o'clock on the clock dial. Place your hands close together. Pull the smoother toward you, scraping the top of the cake. Use a metal spatula to clean up the sides of the cake. After drying, the top will get two or three more coats of icing.

MASTER CHEF'S HINT

Be sure the cake dries thoroughly between each coat of royal icing. Use fine-grade sandpaper to sand away any take-off lines on the cake.

ICING THE CAKE BOARD   Clean up the edges of the cake and the cake board before icing the cake board. Paddle the royal icing onto the cake board using an offset metal spatula, moving the icing up to the bottom edge of the cake. Smooth away some of the icing with the offset spatula. Place a small cardboard on the cake top. This prevents damage to the iced cake.

Place your left hand (if you're right-handed) on the cake board and turn the cake clockwise as far as you can without moving your hand.

With the other hand, position the side or bench scraper at a 45° angle on the cake board at 12 o'clock on the clock dial. The side scraper edge should touch the bottom of the cake edge. Next turn the cake counterclockwise as you move your hands clockwise, icing the board in one turn. Let dry 2 hours. Carefully clean up the bottom edge of the cake.

Lightly sand the cake board for a smoother finish. Ice the cake cardboard once or twice more. You can create an artistic, even marbled look if you wish.

For an added special effect, you can also embellish the royal iced cake board.

The Art of Cake Design

A MASTER CHEF'S SECRETS

CHAPTER 4

Easy Design Techniques

If you feel a little uncomfortable about tackling that fancy cake project, it's good to have a few helpful tools, such as lace presses, stencils, impression stamps, or appliqués, to create pleasing designs relatively quickly and painlessly. Here we provide suggestions about how to create an attractive cake without even picking up a pastry bag. These techniques aren't just for the timid; many cake designers use them every day.

Decorating a cake can be a lot of fun or rather frustrating. The key is to choose a design that's easy enough to execute given your time constraints and abilities. Whether you plan to decorate in royal icing, rolled fondant, model-ing chocolate, or buttercream, we offer a few sure-fire ways to make your cake the object of admiration. You may also want to turn to the appropriate chapter(s) to review particular skills for the kind of icing or other materials you've chosen.

Choosing the Cake

Choosing a cake is the easy part. You probably have a family favorite. If you have a limited time to bake, ice, and decorate the cake, this may not be the best time to try out a recipe you're unfamiliar with. This way, you'll be sure of success. If, on the other hand, you have plenty of time to put this project together, then go ahead and try something that doesn't require too many expensive ingredients. A yellow, chocolate fudge, sponge, or carrot cake can be a good place to begin. You'll also find our scrumptious and versatile cake recipes on pp. 134–151.

Choosing the Icing

The icing on the cake should be delicious. Find my icing recipes on pp. 134–142. Your particular cake design may limit your icing choice; a creamy soft icing can be more difficult to handle than a rolled icing.

If you plan to bring this cake to a family function, tea, or luncheon, then you may prefer a cake with a little more detail work than a cake you'd serve at the dinner table. You can make a white chocolate buttercream icing and swirl it on the cake with an offset metal spatula. Then put white chocolate shavings on top for a delicious and elegant look. Instead of the shavings, you could have a small fresh arrangement of organic flowers on top. Or roll out white modeling chocolate (chocolate plastic or plastique), shape the chocolate into rose petals, and place them on top. A single white chocolate rose would also work nicely.

For a more formal and detailed look, ice a chocolate fudge cake with chocolate fudge icing, amaretto mocha icing, or chocolate pra-

White chocolate roses are fabulous.

line icing. Refrigerate the cake and allow it to become firm. Then roll out ivory or mocha-colored rolled fondant and cover the cake for a perfect finish. If you wish, you could tie the middle of the cake with fabric lace ribbon and add a bow in the center, attached with a dab of royal icing. For a more detailed look, you could use the crimper on the top shoulders of the cake. Or simply leave it plain. You could place a stencil on top of the cake then shake cocoa powder over it or ice the stencil with royal icing. A fresh organic flower arrangement also creates a spectacular look.

Give yourself plenty of time to work on your cake. Often even a simple lovely cake takes a few hours to pull together after you've baked the cake and made the icings and fillings, especially if you don't decorate on a daily basis. If you have enough time, you'll be able to have fun with your design and really enjoy the experience of creating with food.

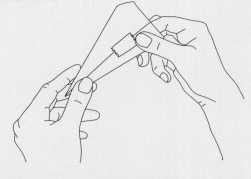

1. With a triangle of parchment paper, bring corner B to meet corner A.

5. Tape the outside seam to secure it.

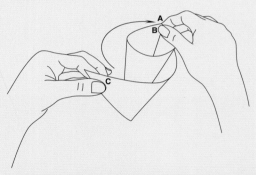

2. Align corner B over corner A.

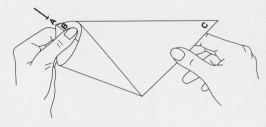

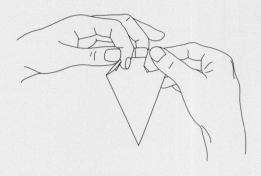

3. Bring corner C around to meet corners A and B. (You may need to change hands to do this.)

6. Fold down the top of the cone.

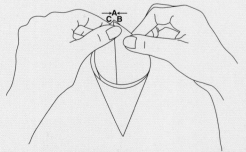

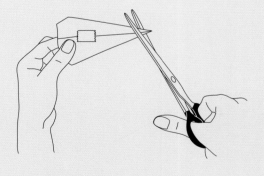

4. Carefully align overlapping corners A, B, and C. Tape the inside seam.

7. Snip a hole at the cone's point. When you're ready, insert the appropriate metal piping tip and load the cone with icing.

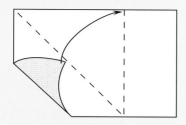

1. Beginning with a rectangle of parchment paper, fold the left corner up to make an equilateral traingle (half of a square).

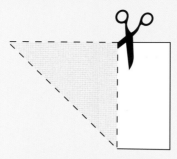

2. Cut off the end.

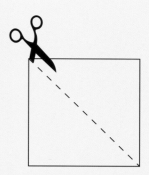

3. Now unfold and cut the two triangles apart.

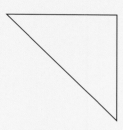

4. Use one of the parchment triangles.

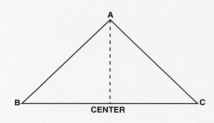

5. Position the triangle like this; note corners A, B, and C.

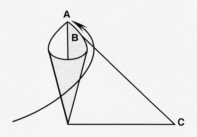

6. Bring corner B up to meet corner A.

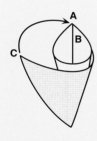

7. Now bring corner C around on the outside to meet corners A and B to complete the cone shape.

8. Make sure that you pull the outside seam (with corner C) as far as it will go. This will help make the cone tight and secure.

9. Seams A and B will be inside and seam C outside. Fold seam A to the outside and seam C to the inside. You will not need to tape the seam.

Cut a small hole at the cone's tip when you're ready to pipe. (The hole will be smaller than that for a metal piping tip.) Use the French parchment cone for icing without a metal piping tip. You can make several of these and have them ready with different colors of icing.

Getting Started

THE PARCHMENT CONE (CORNET)

Parchment paper cones, also known as cornets, are just as necessary as pastry bags. Take care in making them correctly. Keep them on hand in abundance, especially before beginning a cake. You'll need several. Unlike pastry bags, paper cones or cornets are not reusable. We'll talk more about pastry bags in chapter 5, "Buttercream Basics."

MAKING THE STANDARD CONE Cut parchment paper into an equilateral triangle (all three sides measure the same) or buy parchment paper that's already cut into triangles for cones (available at cake-decorating stores). Mark asterisks at the triangle's top, left, and right corners. Put two pieces of masking tape on the back of your opposite writing hand (we'll call it your left hand). With your writing hand (we'll call it your right hand), hold the triangle like a pyramid with the peak (corner A) pointing away from you, or "north" if we were to use a map's N–S–E–W orientation. With your left hand, bring the bottom left corner B up to meet the top corner A or "north" peak. Place corner B directly on top of the north peak A with the ends directly over each other (no overlapping).

Hold the seams of A and B in your right hand. Then with your left hand, bring corner C completely around the cone and up to where corners A and B meet. Make sure that all seams are dead center. All three letters should line up together. Place a piece of tape on the inside seam so that they don't come apart. Fold about 2 inches (5 cm) of flap on the inside. To finish the cone, put a piece of masking tape on the outside seam of the cone. Your parchment-paper cone is ready to be cut, fitted with a tip, and loaded with icing. (See drawings on p. 40.)

THE FRENCH PARCHMENT CONE The French cone is a tightly wrapped parchment-paper cone that's perfect for piping without a metal tip. To create this cone, repeat the procedure for the standard parchment-paper cone up to the point where all of the seams are perfectly aligned at the center. (See pp. 40–41 and below.)

Use your thumb and middle finger to rotate seams B and C in the opposite direction, pulling up on the paper cone as you overlap them. The outside seam (seam C) will lock. This means that the outside seam has gone as far as it can. Stop overlapping here. Fold seam C (the outside seam) inside the paper cone. Seam B is an inside seam. Fold that seam to the outside. Seam A is also an inside seam. Fold that seam to the outside edge.

No masking tape will be needed. Load the bag with a small amount of icing or melted chocolate. Cut a small hole at the tip of the cone when you're ready to pipe.

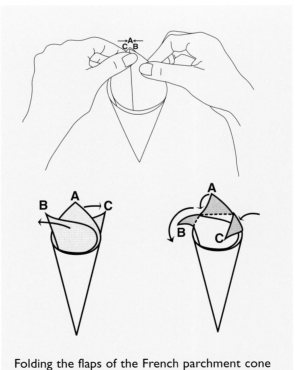

Folding the flaps of the French parchment cone can be a little tricky.

Special Tools & Techniques

CRIMPERS Crimpers are marvelous tools designed for use on cakes with rolled icing. Right after you cover the cake in rolled icing you can crimp the top, sides, or bottom for a no-piping decorative finish. However, you can still add piping to raise certain design elements marked by the crimpers.

You can crimp the top of the cake, pipe Swiss dots on the sides, and tie a wide or thin ribbon around the bottom of the cake. This technique is simple and easy, yet beautiful and effective.

Crimpers are held together with a small black rubber band. This allows you to choose the size of the opening of the crimp. Roll the rubber band forward for a closed look or back for a more open look.

Position the crimper at a 90° angle at the top or middle of the cake. Push the crimper about ⅛ inch into the cake's rolled icing. Squeeze and then release the crimper. Carefully pull the crimper out of the icing and repeat the technique until you have crimped the entire cake. Be careful. Do not pull out the crimper before you release its pressure; otherwise, you'll pull and damage the fondant (rolled icing).

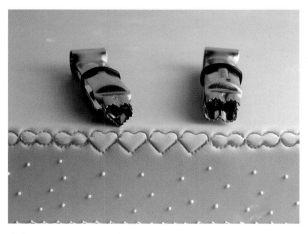

A heart crimper and a crimper with an oval-repeat pattern creates a neat border on rolled fondant.

IMPRESSION STAMPS Impression stamps are a lot easier to use and require a firm cake under the rolled icing. Otherwise, the pressure of pushing the stamp into the rolled icing will damage both the cake and the icing. A pound cake, spice cake, or fruitcake would be ideal.

This impression stamp made this border of flowers and leaves on rolled icing.

Position the stamp anywhere on the cake and apply firm, even pressure. Repeat this procedure until you have completed the design.

Lace & Other Presses

LACE PRESSES Lace presses are all the rage in the world of cake decorating. They can finish a cake in a relatively short time that could take hours to replicate in icing. Many professional cakes are adorned with a variety of lace and other presses. You can buy flexible or hard-plaque presses. Or you can collect inexpensive lace scraps lying around the house to press into cake designs. You'd do this by rubbing a little solid vegetable shortening on the lace. Roll out the fondant on a little cornstarch. Cut the fondant to the desired shape.

Carefully place the lace on the fondant, flat side down. Roll over the lace with a rolling pin. Remove the lace to reveal the lace imprint.

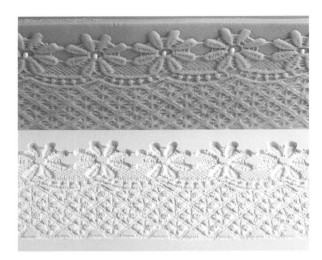

The white plastic lace press (bottom) created the flower and lace design on the pale yellow rolled icing (above).

This press created a simple flower design on rolled fondant that was embellished with piped white royal icing. It sits above the lace-press design.

Some presses come in two parts. This allows a design on the top and bottom of the icing that can later be applied to the cake. Single presses are usually less expensive. To prevent the icing from sticking to the press, knead in ½ teaspoon vegetable shortening for 8 ounces (224 g) of paste.

DOUBLE PRESSES To use a lace press, massage the rolled icing until it's flexible. Add a little vegetable shortening to the rolled icing to prevent the rolled icing from sticking to the press. Flatten out the paste or roll it out to the desired shape and thickness. The paste should be about ¼ inch (6 mm) thick.

If you're using a two-piece press, put the paste in the bottom of the mold and put the top press on. Apply pressure with your full hand or roll a rolling pin over the press. Then pull off the top and pull back the bottom of the press to release the paste with the design.

With a damp pastry brush dipped in water, brush the area where you want to apply the design. (Be sure to remove excess water by brushing the brush against the water container.) Trim the paste's edge and apply it to the cake.

SINGLE PRESSES If using a single press, roll out the paste (rolled icing already worked so that it's pliable and with a little vegetable shortening added) to ¼ inch (6 mm) thick. Put the paste on the press and turn the press over. Apply pressure to the back of the press. Release the paste from the press and trim the excess. Apply the decorative pressed-paste shape to the cake with a dab of water.

DEEP PRESSES Knead extra vegetable shortening into the rolled-icing paste if you are molding a cameo or using a deep wooden press. Shape the paste into a ball and slightly

An acrylic deep-press mold created this cameo.

These metal leaf appliqués function like cookie cutters in creating cutout shapes that you can apply to rolled icing. Note how two sizes of the same leaf shape create a shadow effect. Piped royal icing enhances the design.

flatten it. Push the paste into the press and turn the press over. Apply pressure to the back of the press. Carefully release the paste from the press. Let dry for 30 minutes before trimming the edges. Apply to the cake with a dab of water or royal icing (depending on the depth of the design).

APPLIQUÉS With appliqués, you can decorate a cake simply and quickly. If you add piping on top of the cutout shapes, you can greatly enhance the overall design. However, cutouts alone can make a stunning presentation.

To create this lovely look, dust the surface lightly with cornstarch. Roll out homemade or commercial fondant to ⅛ inch (3 mm) thick. Cut as many shapes as you can in varying sizes. Cover the cutouts with plastic wrap. Reroll scraps and repeat the procedure.

To attach the cutouts, brush the back of the cutout with a little water and attach them to the rolled fondant on the cake. Stagger the cutouts. On some cutouts, place smaller cutouts of the same family in different colors or in hues of one color over each other, attaching them with a little water.

STENCILS Stencils are lovely and easy to use. Available almost anywhere, they are time savers for busy cake designers.

You can stencil almost anything on a cake. You can even make your own stencil and use the stencil on a cake. The icing on the cake generally dictates what medium to use with the stencil, i.e., cocoa powder, confectioners' sugar, royal icing, etc.

For example, we show a child's train that's dusted with cocoa powder (see photo below). This stencil can be placed on a cake iced with

The locomotive stencil (top) created the design (below) for a child's or railroad aficionado's cake. Cocoa powder was sifted over rolled chocolate icing.

buttercream and carefully dusted with cocoa powder sifted with a small sieve over the stencil. You could also ice a cake with rolled icing and sift cocoa powder over the stencil. First, apply a small amount of white vegetable shortening to the top of the cake to be stenciled. This will ensure that the cocoa powder will stay in place after it has been sifted onto the surface.

In another example, we have stenciled a rose with meringue powder royal icing (see photo). You need to have a rolled or hard-drying surface for this technique. Usually a cake iced with rolled fondant, marzipan, or a royal icing will work fine for this technique.

We placed the stencil on the cake, took a small amount of royal icing, and applied it to the stencil at a 45° angle, using a small offset metal spatula or a palette knife. We went over the stencil a couple times to ensure that a uniform amount of icing was used.

Note: You can use buttercream icing to stencil on a rolled surface.

The rose stencil (above) created the design on top of rolled chocolate fondant. Here we applied meringue powder royal icing at a 45° angle. You could use other icings or confectioners' sugar.

Leafy appliqués create an elegant pattern on the sides of this cake.

CHAPTER 5

Buttercream Basics

Perfecting basic buttercream skills makes the difference between nice and wow. In the United States, most cakes intended for special occasions are still iced and decorated with traditional buttercream icing; so mastering buttercream icing and decorating techniques remains extremely important. Even well-trained decorators know that they need to keep abreast of all levels and trends in the decorating arts.

Buttercream piping skills continue to be highly valued. In fact, most American bakeries only offer cakes iced and decorated in buttercream. Here are some of the ways you can use buttercream to create borders, shells and reverse shells, basket weaves, garlands, scrolls, ruffles, swags, bows, rope, zigzags, fleurs-de-lis, rosettes large and small, rosebuds, half-roses, full roses, and other flowers and leaves and leafy designs.

Borders & Flowers

OPEN-STAR TIP

STAR FLOWERS You can use star flowers, piping them with an open-star metal piping tip, in several ways: (1) As a quick technique, you can ice and decorate a cake baked in a character pan; then pipe all the character's features with star flowers. Smoothly ice the sides of the cake with an offset metal spatula. (2) Star flowers are attractive in clusters of three with a center and leaves between the clusters. Pipe these star-flower clusters on cupcakes or cookies, or use small star-flower clusters to adorn a smoothly iced cake. (3) In royal icing, not just buttercream, star flowers can be time-savers for decorating plaques, cookies, and cakes.

To create them, position your open-star tip at a 90° angle. Apply a burst of pressure, extending the icing about ¼ inch (6 mm) beyond the tip. Stop the pressure immediately. Pull the tip

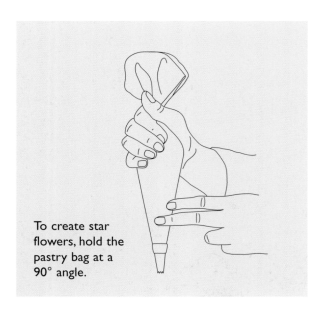

To create star flowers, hold the pastry bag at a 90° angle.

straight up and you'll have a flower with an open center. Complete the flower by piping a tiny dot with a #2 round tip in the flower's center.

To pipe this flower without a center, position your open-star tip at a 90° angle. Apply a burst of pressure, extending the icing about ¼ inch (6 mm) beyond the tip. Gently ease up on the pressure as you slightly raise the metal piping tip. Stop the pressure immediately and pull straight up. You'll see that the flower's center has automatically risen in the middle, so you won't need a center dot to complete the flower.

SHELLS Creating shells is one of the bread-and-butter skills of busy cake decorators. Most cakes iced with buttercream are decorated with shells of one kind or another.

SMALL SHELLS Use small shells for 3-inch to 7-inch (7 to 18 cm) cakes as a top or bottom border. Position the piping tip at a 45° angle at the cake's base. Apply steady and even pressure and squeeze a small amount of icing from the tip, extending about ⅛ inch (3 mm). Push the tip forward while touching the surface, applying steady pressure. After about ¼ inch (6 mm) of icing extends from the tip, pull the tip toward you, easing up on the pressure. Stop the pressure, but continue to pull toward you.

MASTER CHEF'S HINT

As you push and pull to create a small shell, the tip should touch the surface the entire time.

LARGE SHELLS Use large shells for larger cakes. Position the tip at the cake's base. Hold the piping bag between a 45° and 90° angle.

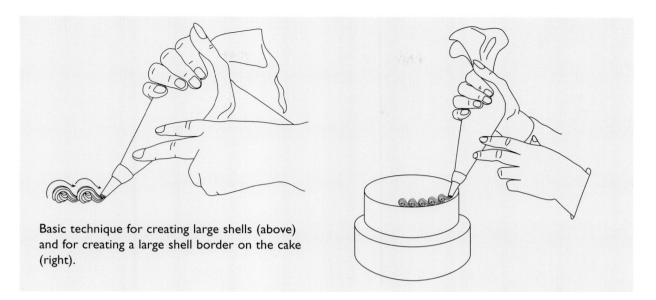

Basic technique for creating large shells (above) and for creating a large shell border on the cake (right).

Raise the tip slightly above the surface. Apply steady and even pressure and squeeze a small amount of icing, extending about ¼ inch (6 mm). Push the tip slightly forward and continue to squeeze until about ½ inch (1.3 cm) of icing extends from the tip. Now, pull the tip toward you, continuing to squeeze as you gently touch the surface. Ease off the pressure and stop, continuing to pull the tip toward you.

Use parchment paper on a hard surface to practice piping with buttercream before decorating the cake. Starting from the top row (left to right) here are strokes for fleur-de-lis, rope, large rosettes, reverse shells, zigzags, zigzags overpiped with shells, small rosettes, large shells, and small shells.

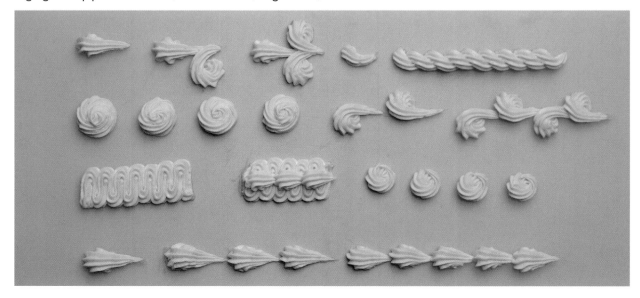

ZIGZAGS Zigzags are generally used as a bottom border. Position the tip at a 45° angle at the base of the cake. Raise the tip slightly off the surface for a puffier border, or drag the tip on the surface for a flatter look. Squeeze the bag and move the tip ½ inch (1.3 cm) to the left or right. Move slightly down while squeezing and move the tip in the opposite direction ½ inch (1.3 cm). Continue this procedure until the design looks like a zigzag.

MASTER CHEF'S HINT

To create a more ornate look, pipe large shells on top of the zigzag.

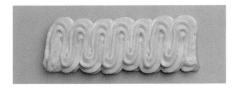

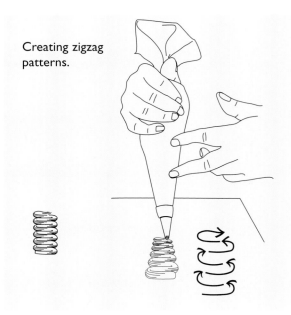

Creating zigzag patterns.

ROSETTES These small flowers look great in a cluster of three with leaves piped in between. Try your hand at small or large rosettes.

SMALL ROSETTES Position the piping tip at a 90° angle, raised slightly above the surface. For a right-handed person, position your hand at 9 o'clock on the clock dial. Squeeze and pipe in a counterclockwise direction one tight rotation. When you return to 9 o'clock, stop the pressure, but continue to move your hand in a counterclockwise direction. This ensures that you don't leave the rosette with a take-off point. For a left-handed person, position your hand at 3 o'clock and pipe one rotation in a clockwise direction. Stop the pressure once you return to 3 o'clock, but continue your hand in a clockwise direction.

LARGE ROSETTES Position the tip at a 90° angle, raised slightly above the cake's surface. For a right-handed person, position your hand at 9 o'clock on the clock dial. Squeeze and pipe in a counterclockwise position in one loose rotation, creating a small space in the rosette's center. When you return to 9 o'clock, move the tip toward the center in a circular motion and gently ease up on the pressure, making sure not to leave a take-off point. Reverse the direction for the left hand.

Large rosettes differ from small rosettes not only in size but technique. The one and a half piping rotation ends in the flower's center.

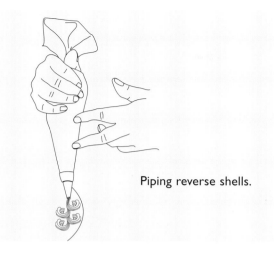

Piping reverse shells.

REVERSE SHELLS

Reverse shells are lovely on the cake's top edge. Position the piping tip at a 45° angle, raised slightly from the cake's surface. Apply pressure and allow ⅛ inch (3 mm) of icing to flow from the tip. Pull back slightly and rotate the tip in a clockwise direction applying even pressure. As you reach 11 o'clock on the clock dial, apply more pressure allowing you to form a curved shape. Start easing-up on the pressure as you pull the piping tip toward you, extending the shell's tail about ½ inch (1.3 cm).

Position the tip to the right of the shell tail. Raise the tip slightly. At a 45° angle, apply pressure and allow ⅛ inch (3 mm) of icing to flow from the tip. Pull back slightly on the tip and rotate the tip in a counterclockwise direction applying even pressure. As you reach 1 o'clock on the clock dial, begin to apply more pressure and allow the pressure to form a curved shape. Ease up on the pressure as you pull the tip toward you and extend the tail of the shell about ½ inch (1.3 cm). Repeat this on the opposite side of the shell tail.

FLEURS-DE-LIS

Fleurs-de-lis can create a lovely border on the cake's top edge and even extend down the sides with drop stringwork. Position the piping tip at a 90° angle. On the top edge of the cake, pipe a large shell and extend the tail between ½ to ¾ inch (1.3 to 1.9 cm). Position the tip to the left of the shell. Starting at the shell's tail, move the tip over ¼ to ½ inch (0.6 to 1.3 cm) to the left and raise the tip ¼ to ½ inch up. At that position, squeeze the bag and allow some icing to flow from the tip. Raise the tip slightly and move the tip in a clockwise direction (forming a rosette). At 11 o'clock on the clock dial, apply more pressure and extend the tail on the top of the centered shell's tail.

Position the piping tip to the right side of the centered shell's tail. Starting at the shell's tail, move the tip over ¼ to ½ inch (0.6 to 1.3 cm) to the right and raise the tip ¼ to ½ inch up. At that position, squeeze the pastry bag and allow some icing to flow from the tip. Raise the tip slightly and move the tip in a counterclockwise direction (forming a rosette). At 1 o'clock on the clock dial, apply more pressure and extend the tail on the top of the centered shell's tail.

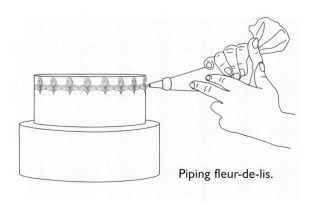

Piping fleur-de-lis.

ROPE Rope can create a beautiful border on the top edge of the cake. It is also used at the bottom of a cake, although that's a little more tricky.

For a right-handed person, raise your piping tip slightly at a 45° angle. Pipe a small curve that looks like an opening quotation mark ("). A left-handed person would make a closing quotation mark ("). Now position the piping tip in the center of the curve held perpendicular to the center. Apply steady pressure as you raise the tip up and end the stroke slightly in front of the first curve. Position the tip in the

center of the curve and continue to make another curve. As you pipe each curve, the finished rope curves will begin to look like an "S" curve.

GARLANDS Garlands create a lush border that gives a cake a sculpted look. This is a side border design that can generally be seen at the top edge of a cake. First, mark your cake to determine how many garlands you will need. A Wilton cake-decorating dividing set is perfect for measuring a cake into many sections. Next pinprick a scalloped shape from one mark to another. This is the pattern that will guide you as you pipe each garland.

Position the piping tip at a 45° angle. Gradually apply pressure to the pastry bag as you pipe in a tight zigzag motion. Slowly build up the pressure as you approach the center of the garland. Now reverse direction and start decreasing pressure as you reach the end of the garland.

MASTER CHEF'S HINT

For a prettier garland, pipe two lines of "strings" on top of the garland. Finish with a tiny bow at each end of the garland or pipe rosebuds.

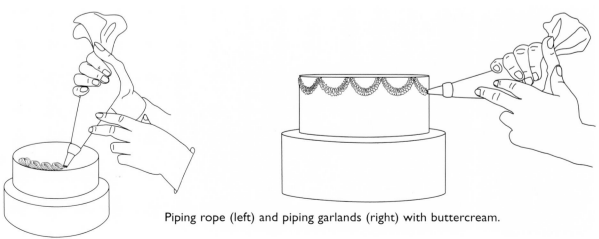

Piping rope (left) and piping garlands (right) with buttercream.

SCROLLS Scrolls are lovely at the top or bottom of a cake. They give the cake a sculpted look. Measure the cake and pinprick scroll patterns on the cake. Position the open-star piping tip at a 45° angle if piping scrolls directly on top of the cake. If piping on the sides, a 90° angle would be appropriate. Raise the tip slightly and squeeze as you follow the outline of the scroll. The tip should slightly drag on the cake surface as you pipe the scroll.

Overpipe the scrolls twice with a #3 round piping tip to give the scroll a thinner look. Now finish the scroll with a #2 round piping tip in a contrasting color.

PETAL-SHAPED TIPS #103 AND 104 ROSEBUDS Rosebuds are pretty and you'll want to make them flawlessly because they're always in demand. Use them for cupcakes, petit fours, cookies, and of course, cakes.

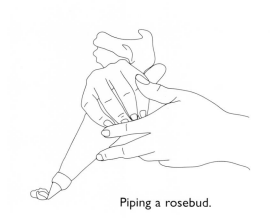

Piping a rosebud.

Position a #103 or #104 petal-shaped metal piping tip at a 45° angle. The wide end of the tip should touch the surface. Slightly pivot the tip to the left if you're right-handed, or to the right if you're left-handed. Squeeze the pastry bag as you rotate the tip to the right, forming a small curve. While the tip is still attached to the icing, raise the tip slightly and move it to the left (about two-thirds the distance of the curve for the petal). Continue to squeeze as you lower the tip and touch the surface at 6 o'clock on the clock dial. Stop the pressure and exit the flower by moving the tip to the right in an upward motion.

Finish the flower by piping the sepal and calyx at the bottom of the flower. To do this, put a small amount of green icing with a #2 round piping tip in a small parchment-paper cone. Position the tip at the bottom of the flower. At the left side, pipe a small upward curve and end at the center. Do the same on the reverse side. Start at the bottom and squeeze the pastry bag and pull in an upward curve. Stop the pressure and pull the tip toward you, leaving the center sepal suspended. Position the tip at the bottom of the flower for the calyx. Finish the flower by applying heavy pressure and then easing off the pressure as you pull a tail about ½ inch (1.3 cm) long.

HALF-ROSES Half-roses are pretty and decorative. Use half-roses along with rosebuds on cookies and cupcakes as well as on cakes.

Follow the procedure for piping the rosebud first. Then, position the #103 or #104 petal-shaped piping tip at a 45° angle at the upper right-hand corner of the rosebud.

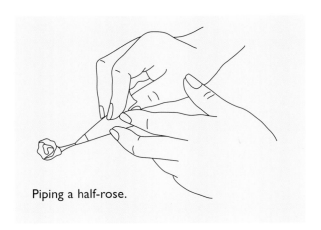

Piping a half-rose.

Tilt the tip to the right. Make sure the wide end of the tip is touching the cake's surface. Apply steady pressure as you drag the tip toward the front of the flower. When you drag the tip to form the petal, start tilting the tip to the left as you overlap the front of the flower. Stop the pressure at the end of the petal. Repeat this procedure for the petal's left side. Remember to tilt the tip to the left before you start to pipe the petal and tilt the tip to the right as you drag the tip to complete the petal. Overlap the left petal over the right petal.

Complete the half-rose by piping the sepals and calyx exactly as you did for the rosebud.

HALF-ROSES (SECOND VARIATION) This beautiful variation creates an over-the-top half-rose. First, start with the rosebud. Second, pipe the right petal by positioning the #103 or #104 petal-shaped piping tip at the upper right-hand corner of the rosebud. Make sure that the wide end of the tip is touching the surface. Squeeze the pastry bag as you drag the tip to form a "G" clef. The petal should be extremely tight to the rosebud. Slightly overlap the petal. Stop the pressure. Now position the tip in the upper left-hand corner. Repeat the procedure for the right petal, only drag the tip to form a tight "C." Drag the tip and overlap the left petal over the right petal.

For the last petal, position the piping tip slightly below the upper right-hand corner of the flower. Tilt the tip to the right and drag it to the front of the flower. As you drag the tip, begin tilting the tip to the left. Cross over the front of the flower and continue to drag the tip to the upper left-hand corner of the flower. Stop the pressure and gently pull away. Pipe sepals and calyx.

MASTER CHEF'S HINT

For success in piping half-roses, keep the tip extremely close to the flower when piping the last petal. The flower only looks right after you complete the sepals and calyx.

RUFFLES Ruffles are pretty as a border or side design. Try the #88 piping tip to create beautiful ruffles along with zigzags on the top to finish the ruffles.

Position the #103 or #104 petal-shaped piping tip at a 45° angle. Make sure the wide end of the tip touches the surface. Apply pressure as you move the tip in an up-and-down motion, pulling the tip toward you. The more even the pressure, the prettier the ruffles. The same applies to the #88 tip. Put the wide-end piping tip (the star-shape part) on the cake's surface. Apply pressure in an up-and-down motion to form ruffles.

SWAGS Swags are lovely on the sides or top edge of the cake. First, mark the cake to determine the number of swags to pipe. Pinprick a scalloped pattern to be used as a guide. Position the wide end of the #103 or #104 petal-shaped tip touching the surface. Lightly drag the piping tip from one point to another. Make sure that the tip lightly touches the surface as you drag it.

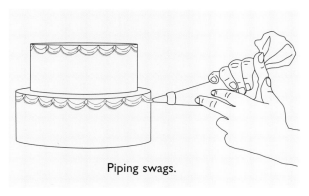

Piping swags.

BOWS A bow can be a pretty finish to a bouquet of flowers or create a pretty trim for a little girl's cake. Position the #103 or #104 petal-shaped piping tip at a 45° angle. Position the wide end of the tip on the surface. Drag the tip as you apply steady pressure, making a figure "8." Start with the left loop first; move the tip up and around. When you return to the home position, move the tip up and around to the right. Once you're back at the home position, drag the tip and taper off the icing to form the left streamer. Reposition the tip at the home position. Drag the tip and taper off the icing to form the right streamer.

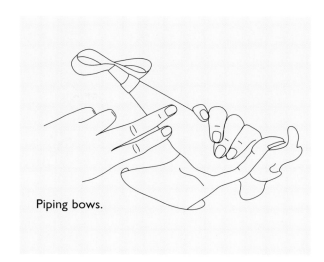

Piping bows.

BASKET WEAVE, LEAF AND ROUND TIPS #4 TO 10, 47, 48, 67, AND 352

BASKET WEAVES A basket weave creates a stunning tailored finish that even beginners can master. It doesn't matter if you're not yet proficient enough at smoothly icing a cake. First, pipe a straight line with a #4 or #5 round piping tip or a #18 star tip, or a #47 or #48 basket-weave tip. Your position would be 90° if piping on the sides of a cake. If piping on top of the cake, the tip position would be 45°.

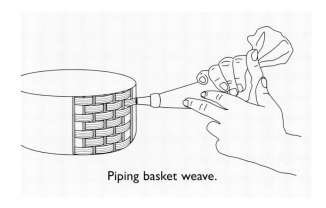

Piping basket weave.

After piping a straight line from the top to the bottom of the cake, pipe horizontal strips of lines ½ inch (1.3 cm) before the line and ½ inch (1.3 cm) after the line. The next line is the "tip space." The tip space is the same width as

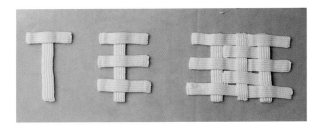

the icing strip, but left empty until you pipe another vertical strip. Pipe the second, third, fourth, etc. horizontal strips. Next pipe another vertical strip. Make sure that you align the vertical strip with the horizontal strips. Finally, pipe horizontal strips in the tip space and extend the strips to ½ inch (1.3 cm) long. Repeat this technique until you have woven the sides of the cake.

The basket weave was made with buttercream. The petals and fruit were shaped from marzipan, and the flowers from rolled fondant.

LEAF TIPS Leaf tips make a nice finish to a cluster of flowers. The #352 leaf piping tip is an easy and quick way to pipe leaves. The #67 leaf piping tip is also popular. The former requires less fuss and technique. With the #352 tip, position the (narrow or wide) end of the tip at a 45° angle.

Apply a burst of pressure on the pastry bag and drag the tip to a finish. With the #67 leaf tip, hold the pointed edge at a 45° angle and apply a burst of pressure on the pastry bag. Build up the head of the leaf first; then pull the tip toward you to end with a point. If the tip does not end in a point, use a toothpick to pull the ends together.

MASTER CHEF'S HINT

When piping leaves with the #67 leaf tip, add a little more liquid to buttercream icing for a softer consistency.

ROUND TIPS Round piping tips are among my favorites, especially when piping fine work. The larger tips are also as important because they can be a nice change from the usual shells at the bottom of the cake.

To use the #7, #8, #9, or #10 metal piping tips for border work, position the tip at a 45° angle. Squeeze the pastry bag and allow a little icing to extend from the tip. Push the tip forward (building the size of the oval) as you squeeze and then pull the tip, easing up on the pressure to form an oval shape. Stop the pressure and pull toward yourself. To start the next oval, position the tip ¼ inch (6 mm) from the previous oval and repeat the technique.

#103 AND 104 TIPS

FULL-BLOWN ROSES Perhaps roses are the flower most widely used on cakes. Piped roses are as American as apple pie. A bakery cake isn't complete until piped roses adorn it. While roses are used in abundance, piped roses have suffered greatly. Perhaps this unique way of piping roses will make them easier to create and more accessible to busy decorators.

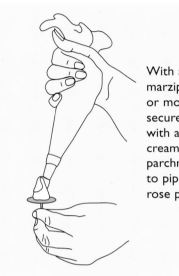

With a cone made of marzipan, rolled fondant, or modeling chocolate secured to an icing nail with a dot of buttercream on a square of parchment paper, begin to pipe the first inside rose petal.

Instead of piping cones out of buttercream or royal icing to support the rose, hand-model cones out of marzipan, rolled fondant, or white or dark modeling chocolate (chocolate plastic). That way, you can make the cones days, weeks, or months ahead. (Refrigerate marzipan bases until you're ready to use them.)

Attach a little buttercream to the icing nail. Use a #6 or #7 icing nail. Put a small 2x2-inch (5x5-cm) square of parchment or wax paper on the nail. Put a dot of buttercream in the center of the paper to hold the cone. Place the cone on the buttercream.

Position the #103 or #104 petal-shaped piping tip at a 90° angle to the cone. The wide end of the tip should be touching the right side of the cone (at 3 o'clock or 9 o'clock on the clock dial) and about ½ inch (1.3 cm) down from the tip of the cone.

MASTER CHEF'S HINT

Both left-handed and right-handed cake designers pipe in either direction when piping the rose. For clarity here, I begin with the tip at 3 o'clock on the clock dial.

Squeeze the pastry bag loaded with buttercream and raise the piping tip steadily (about ¼ inch or 6 mm above the tip of the cone). Begin to turn the icing nail counterclockwise as you wrap a layer of icing over the tip of the cone. Once you overlap the icing, gradually ease off the pressure and pull the tip down, touching the sides of the cone. This is the first petal.

For the next three petals, position the piping tip at the overlapped seam. This time hold the tip at a 45° angle with the tip's wide end touching the seam. Position the tip about ½ inch (1.3 cm) from the top of the cone and at

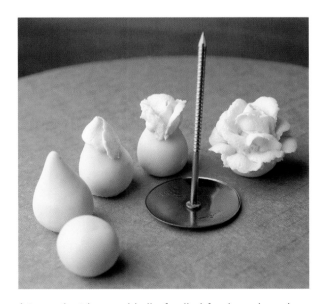

Icing nail with round ball of rolled fondant, shaped into a cone, and progressive stages of adding buttercream petals.

3 o'clock on the clock dial. Slightly tilt the tip to the right. Apply even pressure in the pastry bag as you turn the icing nail counterclockwise and raise the tip up and down to form the next petal. Stop the pressure. Continue with the next petal, starting where you left off using the same technique as raising the tip up and down as you turn the icing nail. Now, pipe the last petal and end where the first petal began. You now have a rosebud.

For the next five petals, position the tip at any seam or at the center point of any one petal. The tip should be slightly under the previous petals. At a 45° angle, tilt the tip slightly to the right. Squeeze as you raise the tip and petal up to the mid-point of the previous petal and down. Remember to turn the icing nail counterclockwise. Position the tip slightly in back of the petal you just piped (to overlap). Repeat the same technique to pipe the next petal.

Continue until you pipe a total of five overlapping petals. For the last seven petals, tilt the uncompleted rose to the left as you tilt the piping tip to the right (to get under the petal). Position the tip at the center of one of the petals. With the tip's wide end touching, pipe seven overlapping petals. The rose is complete. If you didn't use up the space of the cone, don't worry. You can cut that off when the rose is dry or leave it on and pipe leaves in between a cluster of roses to hide the bases.

MASTER CHEF'S HINT

Remember to drag the tip lightly to the cone. This way, the petal won't fall off the cone.

CHAPTER 6

Royal Icing Design Skills

Royal icing piping techniques are more difficult than those for buttercream, but you can master them with a lot of practice. And the results are exciting. With royal icing you can create freehand or brush embroidery, learn to outline and flood shapes, add Swiss dots, use hail spotting, or enhance a design with satin stitching. Try your hand at overpiping on "V," scallop, or half-circle shapes. Or create lattices and cushion lattices, top and bottom designs, fleurs-de-lis, lilies-of-the-valley, ruffles, shells, scrolls, and zigzags. We'll also show you bridge and extension work, sometimes known as stringwork.

Focus on one technique at a time and give yourself permission to make plenty of mistakes. That's how we all learned.

Embroidery Piping

Embroidery piping is a wonderful place to begin to develop and perfect your fine royal-icing skills. So that you're not overwhelmed, we've grouped embroidery piping techniques into freehand embroidery, brush embroidery, satin stitching, cornelli lace, piped lace, pyramid stitching, and finally, artistic freehand embroidery in which you create your own patterns and designs. Use the appropriate metal piping tip in a parchment cone or pastry bag.

FREEHAND EMBROIDERY Freehand embroidery and piping, as well as bridge and extension work, are hallmarks of Australian-style cake decorating. At first, it seems impossible to pipe this freehand. Yet the more you do it, the more logical it seems. Actually, all freehand embroidery is made up of tiny curves and punctuation marks, like periods, exclamation marks, commas, open and closed quotation marks, circles and ovals, and little "S" and "C" curves. Once you understand that, the rest is feeling comfortable piping these curvy shapes directly on the cake. It's helpful to mark the cake to determine the size and spacing of the embroidery so that everything looks even.

Begin by practicing small circles and ovals. (Practice your piping on parchment paper or cardboard on a hard surface.) The difficult part will be working with a #0 metal piping tip and perfectly consistent royal icing. One key element to remember is to drag the tip lightly on the surface when piping freehand embroidery. This will give you the control. You should practice holding the piping tip at a 45° angle if you're working on a flat, hard surface.

MASTER CHEF'S HINT

The smaller the paper cone or pastry bag, the more control you'll have using a #0 metal piping tip.

Next make those circles and ovals into a pattern to form a flower. Then practice commas and periods in a curved motif. Your embroidery should have a natural form to it and not look straight. However, it should appear as though a pattern were used. Draw a pattern of embroidery piping that you would like; then practice it just by looking at the pattern. After you have practiced it enough, mark and measure the cake. Apply the piping directly to the cake.

Practice long curved lines and pulling out stems from those lines. Then practice creating a lily bud by squeezing a small ball of icing from the pastry bag. Before you exit the bud, continue to squeeze the icing from the parchment cone and pull out a stem to the left of the bud; then insert the tip back into the bud and squeeze the bag and pull a stem out to the right.

To practice freehand embroidery, first try making small circles and ovals. Use ovals, circles, or dots to build a flower and elaborate. Then practice making short and long curvy lines.

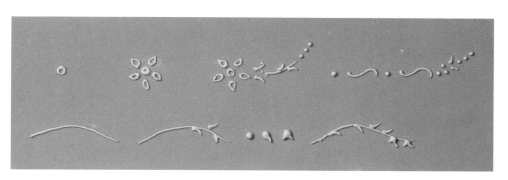

Here are steps for freehand embroidery of lily of the valley.

For the lily-of-the-valley flower, you'll need a #84, #80, or #79 piping tip (for a larger flower) and a small bag with royal icing. Hold the piping tip at a 45° angle. Rotate the tip from left to right as you squeeze the pastry bag and pull slightly off to the right. Now practice using curves, lines, dots, circles, and commas to form a pretty embroidery pattern.

BRUSH EMBROIDERY This is an easy technique but one that requires practice to truly perfect. The results are absolutely stunning. And when you incorporate brush embroidery with freehand embroidery, your cake will now appear like a work of art.

First, transfer the pattern (like the one on p. 159) to the surface. To do this, trace the pattern using see-through paper. Also trace the back of the pattern. Turn the pattern right side up and put the pattern on a hard dried surface. Retrace the pattern with a #2 graphite pencil. A copy of the pattern will be revealed on the hard surface, whether it's a cake covered with marzipan or rolled fondant or a plaque made of pastillage or marzipan.

See how you can build up a flower shape with brush embroidery.

Next fill a small parchment paper cone with royal icing and a #2 or #3 metal round tip. Start from the outline and work to the center of the design. Outline the first petal or leaf. Before the outline dries, use a damp paintbrush to brush the outline icing toward the base of the petal or leaf. Use long strokes as you brush the icing. Don't completely brush the outline icing away. Leave the bulk of the outline intact. When you brush, you'll see some of the surface through the brushed icing. Dampen the brush with water or pasteurized egg whites. Egg whites will leave a nice shine.

Go on to the next petal and do the same. You can only brush one petal or leaf at a time. Otherwise, the outline will become dry. After you've brushed the petals and leaves and they've dried, pipe veins in the leaves with a #0 piping tip and royal icing. Start at the base of the leaf and drag the icing in a long curve toward the leaf's tip. Go back to the curve and pull out tiny lines. For the center of the flower, pipe a cluster of dots with the #0 piping tip.

SATIN STITCH The satin stitch is a lovely design for dressing up a cake. It is most effective on a flooded monogram where the raised piping resembles carefully woven thread. Most often the satin stitch is piped directly on a cake covered with marzipan or rolled fondant.

For monograms with a raised look, carefully trace the pattern on see-through paper. If the surface is dry, you can use this tracing method to transfer it. Trace the back of the pattern with a #2 graphite pencil. Now turn the pattern over to its correct side and place it on the dry surface. Carefully retrace the pattern. Remove the pattern. You'll have a carbon copy of the pattern. Using meringue powder royal icing, outline the pattern and

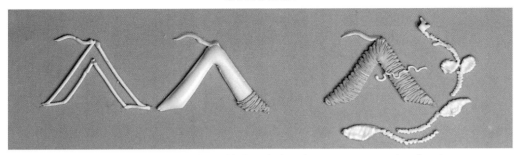

The "A" monogram was outlined (far left), flooded with meringue powder flood icing (center), and satin stitched. Then the monogram was embellished with freehand embroidery.

carefully flood the monogram. (See "Flooding Techniques.") Let dry for 2 to 4 hours before applying the satin stitch. (See photo above.)

When you're ready to satin stitch, put a #0 metal piping tip into a medium-size paper cone. Half-fill the pastry bag with meringue powder royal icing. Start at the top or bottom of the monogram. Pipe zigzag lines very close to each other in a back-and-forth motion.

MASTER CHEF'S HINT

If the surface is soft and you want to transfer a pattern, place the traced pattern on the soft surface. Use a straight pin to pinprick the monogram onto the soft surface. Remove the pattern to reveal the pinprick design. Outline and flood the design.

Flooding Techniques

This is a fast and easy way to create one- and two-dimensional designs using royal icing in two consistencies. With flooding techniques, you can pipe monograms or greetings on cakes, create collars, and fashion decorative motifs. Flood icing can even be used to build bridges during bridge and extension work (also called stringwork). Flood icing variations can be used when creating Swiss dots or hail spots.

OUTLINING AND FLOODING First, outline the design to be flooded. You can use meringue powder royal icing and flood icings to do this. You can also use egg-white royal icing with flood icing. Put a small amount of flood icing into a medium-size paper cone. Make sure the cone has no hole. Then, carefully cut a small hole (about the size of a #2 or #3 metal round piping tip). Starting at the top of the design, squeeze the pastry bag gradually, keeping the bag tip inside the icing as you squeeze. Quickly move the bag as you gradually squeeze. Keep the bulk of the icing in the center of the outline. Stop squeezing. Insert a toothpick and quickly move the icing to the perimeter of the outline. Don't be stingy when flooding a piece. You want a slightly puffy look to the outline. If you outlined with a #2 or #3 piping tip, the outline icing will hold the flood icing. Let dry for 2 to 4 hours for a small piece or 6 to 12 hours for a very large piece.

SWISS DOTS Creating Swiss dots is perhaps the easiest technique used to decorate a cake. Royal icing piped onto the cake forms the small dots. The key to this technique is to soften the royal icing with a little water or pasteurized egg white. If you don't, the dots will form peaks as you pull the tip of the bag away from the cake. If the icing is softened, the peaks will settle back to a round shape. To check if the icing is the right consistency, take an offset metal spatula and dip it into the royal icing (with a little water added). Touch the surface lightly and pull up the spatula. If the icing rolls back to a small ball and holds its shape, it is the correct consistency. If a peak forms at the top of the icing, you need to add more water.

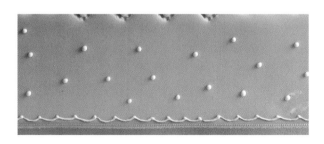

Next take a small amount of softened royal icing and place it in a small paper cone without a piping tip. Cut a tiny hole in the pastry bag. Squeeze with light pressure at a 90° angle to form a small ball on the surface. Pull the bag away. The peak settles back into a rounded ball.

Bridge & Extension Work

Bridge and extension work, also known as stringwork, is the hallmark of classic Australian-style cake decorating. To create it, little lines of royal icing are piped through a #0 metal piping tip, extending from the lower third of the cake to the bottom of the cake "bridge." This style is one of my favorites, in part because of the discipline required to execute this style beautifully.

MARKING THE CAKE Mark the cake by using a strip of adding machine paper around the cake's circumference. Fold the strip as many times as necessary to create equal sections. Fold the paper in half, then in half again to make fourths, then in half again to make sixteenths.

MARKING THE CAKE

Measure the height of the folded strips to create even sections.

CAKE HEIGHT	STRIP HEIGHT
3 inches	1¼ inches
4 inches	1½ inches
5 inches	1¾ inches

Cut off the excess height of the adding-machine paper. Using a round cookie cutter or a wine glass, position the cutter at one end of the strip and draw a curve from one edge of the strip to the other. Carefully cut on the curved line. Unfold the strip of paper and attach the paper around the circumference of the cake—raising the paper approximately ¼ inch (6 mm) from the bottom of the cake. Secure the paper around the cake with a little masking tape or with a straight pin.

Score the top edge of the paper with a trac-

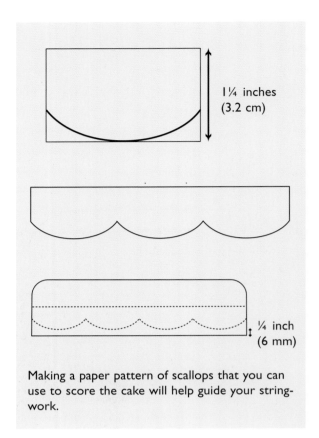

1¼ inches
(3.2 cm)

¼ inch
(6 mm)

Making a paper pattern of scallops that you can use to score the cake will help guide your string-work.

EXTENSION WORK Sieve a small amount of royal icing through a nylon stocking or use an offset metal spatula to smash the icing against a flat surface to get rid of any lumps of sugar. Cut a small parchment-paper cone and fit with a PME #0 metal piping tip. Add up to 1 tablespoon of royal icing to the paper cone and close.

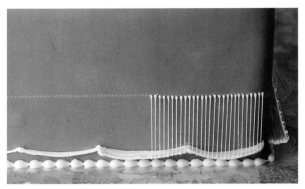

Note the scalloped bridge along the bottom of the cake about ¼ inch up from the bottom beading.

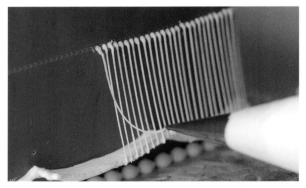

When piping an extension, hold the string for several seconds to measure it and allow it to air dry.

Hail spotting enhances stringwork (also called bridge and extension work).

ing wheel (where the extension work begins). Then, score the scalloped bottom of the paper (where the bridge work ends). Remove the paper.

MAKING THE BRIDGE If desired, pipe a snail trail or oval border, using a #5 or #6 round piping tip around the bottom of the cake. Using a #2 or #3 round piping tip, pipe the first row of the scalloped bridge (using the mark made by the tracing wheel as a guide). After you have gone completely around the cake, pipe the next row parallel to the first row. Build up the piped lines in between five to seven times. Let lines dry between each row.

To smooth the bridge—take some flood icing and brush over the bridge to cover any cracks and spaces between the bridge's foundation. Let dry for 2 to 4 hours.

Starting at the top of the scored line, position the piping tip at the top of the line and touch the cake. Apply a burst of pressure to the paper cone at the start, creating a dot; then squeeze and pull the piping tip upward, carefully assessing the length of the distance from the top of the line to the bottom of the bridge. Hold the string for a brief moment to slightly air dry the icing. Then, bring the tip to the bottom of the bridge and break the icing off at the bridge or move the piping tip slightly under the bridge to break off the icing.

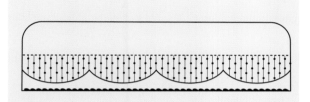

Stringwork and hail spotting along the bottom half of the cake.

The next line should be between $1/16$ to $1/8$ inch (1.5 to 3 mm). Continue until you complete the stringwork.

HAIL SPOTTING Hail spots are similar to Swiss dots, except they are a lot smaller. The icing consistency for both techniques is the same. Take some softened egg white royal icing (between piping consistency and flooding consistency). Put 1 teaspoon of icing in a small paper cone (without a tip). With scissors, snip a tiny hole at the end of the cone. Position the paper cone's tip at the top of the stringwork and squeeze the cone, letting the icing—and not the cone—touch the stringwork. Carefully space the dots on the line. Do this to every other line or every 3 lines.

BRIDGE AND EXTENSION WORK VARIATIONS To create "side curtains" drawn to the sides of standard stringwork, you'll need to build an additional bridge on top of an existing bridge. Carefully repipe 5 or 6 additional lines to the existing bridge with stringwork. Or, create another type of bridge by piping gradual lines, starting in the middle of the bridge and alternately piping lines from the left and right

STRINGWORK VARIATIONS

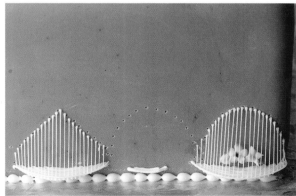

that overlap the centered line. This is called a beveled bridge. This technique builds a bridge, but avoids any built-up piping between sections of bridgework.

For side curtains, when working on the right side of the bridge, tilt the cake to the left. A tilting turntable would be ideal, or simply put a small object under the left side of the cake to achieve the same result. It's also helpful to raise the cake up to a comfortable elevation by putting a couple of books under it. Starting in the center at the top of the stringwork, pipe 6 lines from the top of the stringwork to the new bridgework. Repeat this technique for the left side of the bridge.

Finally, classic stringwork would seem incomplete without lace pieces attached to the top. You can add them by putting a piece of plastic film over a pattern of traced lace. Secure the plastic wrap with masking tape, making the plastic taut. With a #0 metal piping tip, outline the lace pieces, slightly dragging the tip when piping the pieces. Let the iced lace dry for several hours. Carefully cut out sections of the lace pieces and carefully pull them over a table edge to release the lace from the iced pieces.

Pipe dots of royal icing slightly above the stringwork and then delicately and carefully put your thumb underneath the lace piece and your index finger on top of the lace to place it; stick the lace to the dots of royal icing. Keep your fingers on the lace for a few seconds to allow the lace pieces to dry in place. Repeat this until you have attached all the desired lace pieces around the cake.

This elaborate Victorian-style cake (photo right) illustrates masterful overpiping techniques popularized by Joseph A. Lambeth.

Overpiping Techniques

In the 1890s to 1920s, overpiping cake-decorating techniques became popular. The raised, three-dimensional decoration created cakes that resembled large Victorian vases and sculpted works of art, made famous by its best known practitioner, Joseph A. Lambeth, father of cake decorating. Today we rarely see cakes decorated in an ornate overpiping style. I am happy to present a few of these lavish techniques, which are in a class by themselves.

Overpiping uses royal icing as its chief element. Gumpaste and pastillage pieces are added to make the cakes resemble hand-

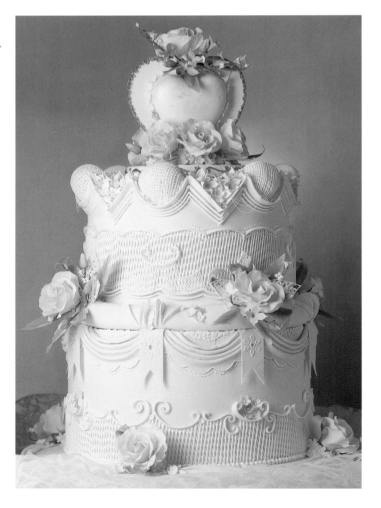

sculpted masterpieces. We can adapt some techniques used in buttercream to make this decorating style more accessible. Practice, practice, practice is the key to getting a steady hand to pipe one line directly over another in various curves and shapes. This style demands a lot of time to complete the cakes. Often fruitcakes, covered with marzipan then iced with royal icing, are decorated with overpiping. Actually, you can spend weeks or months decorating the cake by overpiping.

"V" SHAPES AND SCALLOPS Overpiped "V" shapes and scallops are useful when you are planning to put piped or hand-shaped flowers inside the cavity of the built-up lines. These overpiped shapes are generally found near the cake's top edge. They can also be used as a support garland for "cushion lattice" which are puffs of crisscross lines built up to resemble a lattice ball.

Begin by carefully measuring your cake. Use adding-machine paper to measure around the cake's circumference and divide the paper into sections, or use a Wilton cake dividing set to divide and measure different sections of the

First create "V" shapes or scallops; then overpipe to create dimension. Inside the cavity of the built-up lines you can pipe or position hand-shaped flowers.

cake. Measure from the top of the cake to the peak of the design. Use a pencil mark or pin-prick at these key points so that you will have a guide with piping.

Tilt your cake up by placing a small piece of Styrofoam or a small object under the cake (at 6 o'clock on the clock dial). If you have a tilting turntable, tilt the cake to almost a 45° angle. Fill a pastry bag with royal icing and start with a #4 or #5 metal round piping tip. Pipe "V's" or scallops all around the cake. If you are building up several lines of piping, you can pipe another line directly on top of the previous line. Continue until you have gone completely around the cake. Let this dry for 1 to 2 hours. The more you allow this to dry, the easier it will be to add more lines. Also, if you make a mistake, it's easier to remove the mistake when the previous lines are already dry.

Pipe two to three lines with a #4 or #5 piping tip. Then, change to a #3 metal round piping tip. Pipe two to three more lines, letting the lines dry for 1 hour between each line. Then change to a #2 metal round piping tip and pipe two lines. For a deeper and more sculpted look, add a little color to the royal icing (preferably a contrasting color) and pipe the last line with the #2 metal round piping tip with a deeper color.

Now pipe lines directly below the "V" shapes and scalloped curves and repeat the technique of built-up lines. However, you want to decrease the number of lines as you build down. For example, the first "V" or scallop (the scallop shape or curve resembles a half circle) can have 6 to 8 lines. The line below it will have two lines less, and the line below that two lines less until you reach the last line that only has a single line piped with a #2 piping tip.

Let everything dry before you add any piped or hand-molded flowers inside the cavities.

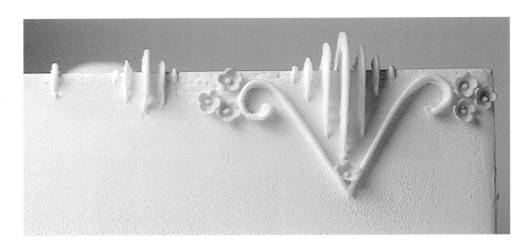

"V" and half-circle shapes embellished with vertical piped lines and flowers create a lovely border.

HALF-CIRCLE SHAPES Half-circles are beautiful and stately if piped accurately. Generally, cake designers pipe these from the top of the cake and extend them down the cake's sides. The center curve, which is the largest curve, gets the most lines. The lines from the left and right of the center curve are decreased by two lines, and so forth as the piped lines spread.

First pipe three small curves with a #4 metal round piping tip, adding two more lines to the center curve. Let dry for 30 minutes. Pipe another line over all three curves. Let dry 1 hour. Now pipe one line to the left and right of the three curves. Pipe an additional line on the three curves. Let dry for 1 hour. Change to a #2 piping tip. Pipe a line on all the curves. Let dry for 1 hour. Then pipe a new line to the left and right of the five curved lines with a #2 piping tip. Pipe lines on the five curved lines. Let them dry.

You can create any type of pattern and pipe as many lines as you like to create depth.

LATTICE For this simple and beautiful lattice technique, accuracy and uniformity are important. First, load a pastry bag with a #3 or #4 round metal piping tip. If the latticework is a part of a "C" or "S" scroll design, begin the initial "C" or "S" scroll design first. Don't build up the scrolls yet. Next start the lattice piping. Lift up the cake and put a small object under the cake to tilt it to the right. Starting at the left side of the cake, pipe straight lines at an angle. After you complete the lines at one angle, let them dry for 1 hour. This time, put a small object under the cake to tilt the cake to the left. Begin to pipe lines in the opposite direction, crisscrossing the lines.

After you've piped all the lines, build up the "C" or "S" scroll scallop above the lattice lines.

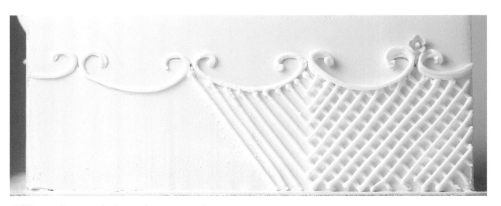

"C" scrolls piped above lattice work.

For cushion lattice, begin with a built-up center (far left). Then begin to add lines, piped in rows crisscrossing over each other. The lines will create a round shape over the raised center. For a finish, you could pipe leaves or flowers around the cushion lattice.

CUSHION LATTICE The cushion lattice makes a stunning border, considered to be the hallmark of overpiped techniques. The key to success is time and patience. For the lattice, lines of royal icing crisscross over a built-up center. The lines must dry between each set of piped lines, starting with a larger round piping tip and ending with a smaller round piping tip.

MASTER CHEF'S HINT

Begin the first crisscross line in the center of the scalloped puff. Then pipe to the right, then to the left of the line. This will help you stay on track when crisscrossing the lines.

First, bevel the cake by cutting off the cake's top edge with a pair of scissors. Your cut should be ½ to ¾ inch (1.3 to 2 cm) on the top inside edge of the cake and ½ to ¾ inch on the top sides of the cake. Ice with marzipan and several coats of royal icing. Next measure space for cushion lattice. If you are piping this around an 8-inch diameter round cake, allow for five to six cushions. For a 10-inch (25-cm) diameter cake, seven to eight cushions, and so forth. Put a #18 or #199 open-star piping tip into a pastry bag with egg-white royal icing. Squeeze an oval puff of icing into each measured space. This creates the foundation. The puff should measure about 1 inch (2.5 cm) long. Don't be afraid to squeeze the pastry bag to puff up the foundation. Let it dry for 3 hours.

With a #5 round metal piping tip in a pastry bag, pipe lines starting at an angle at the cake's left side. Now pipe lines in the opposite direction. Let them dry for 1 hour. Repeat the lines, piping directly on top of the previous lines. You have now piped "one set." Let the set dry for 3 to 6 hours. After they're dry, pipe another set, using the same piping tip. Let them dry for 3 to 6 hours. Now switch to a #3 round piping tip and pipe two sets, drying between each set. Finally, switch to a #1 metal piping tip and pipe two sets.

Border Designs

These various border designs work nicely on the top, sides, or bottom of the cake. Except for stringwork and a few exacting techniques, you could pipe many of these designs with buttercream icing. Everything in this chapter is designed for royal icing. Royal icing creates a clean, perfected look and is most desirable when the cake has been iced in marzipan, rolled fondant, or royal icing. The results are beautiful and well worth the effort of consistent practice.

Reverse shells with scalloped strings, finished with "M" shapes below.

Shells with "S" scrolls just below them.

Garlands with stringwork.

Fleurs-de-lis with overpiping and stringwork.

TOP BORDER DESIGNS

REVERSE SHELLS WITH SCALLOPED STRINGS This is one of my favorite borders. I usually create reverse shells with scalloped strings out of buttercream icing. First, pipe reverse shells on top of the cake with a #18 star metal piping tip. Next carefully measure the cake and pipe scalloped strings under the reverse shells with a #3 or #4 round piping tip. Complete this design by piping fine embroidery ("M" shapes) under the scalloped strings.

SHELLS WITH "S" SCROLLS Shells with "S" scrolls make a lovely and balanced top border. Pipe large shells around the top of the cake with a #18 metal piping tip. Next measure the cake and pipe "S" scrolls under the shells. To complete this design, overpipe the scrolls with a contrasting color to give them depth.

GARLANDS WITH STRINGS For garlands with strings, measure the cake carefully. Pipe garlands around the cake with a #18 metal piping tip. Next pipe drop strings on top of the scallop—one in the middle and one slightly below the middle of the garland. To finish the design, pipe one or two drop strings below the garlands for added depth.

FLEURS-DE-LIS WITH OVERPIPING AND DROP STRINGS This is classical piping in all its glory. Many American cakes were decorated in this popular style, along with scalloped ruffles and garland work, in the 1960s and early 1970s. First, measure cake for the fleurs-de-lis. Pipe the border with a #18 star metal piping tip. For a larger fleur-de-lis, use a #20 or #21 star metal piping tip. Next overpipe strings on the fleurs-de-lis with a #2 round piping tip. Finally, pipe drop strings, connecting one fleur-de-lis to another.

Bottom Border Designs

ZIGZAGS WITH LARGE SHELLS Zigzags with large shells create a beautiful bottom border. Pipe zigzags with a #18 star piping tip. Next pipe large shells with the same tip over the zigzag. Finally, pipe reverse scallops above the shells with a #2 round piping tip directly on the cake and tiny embroidery "U" shapes above the scallops.

SHELLS WITH SCALLOPS Shells with scallops is an easy border. With the addition of embroidery, this border transforms a cake into a work of art. First, pipe large shells with a #18 star piping tip. Next pipe scallops with a #2 round piping tip above the shells. The scallops should be touching the cake. Overpipe the scallops in a contrasting color for more depth. Finally, pipe some fine embroidery with a #1 piping tip. Pipe the "U" embroidery directly on the cake inside the scallop shape.

RUFFLES Ruffles create one of the most beautiful borders for cakes. Most of the time, ruffles are arranged in scallop shapes around the cake's top edge. I use them as a bottom border to give a lovely, feminine appearance to the cake. There are two looks to ruffles, one with a #104 or #88 petal-shaped piping tip. The #104 piping tip gives a finer ruffle, but the back edge is not finished. The #88 piping tip produces a heavier ruffle, but it gives a flawless zigzag finish to the back of the ruffles. Review the procedures for piping ruffles. Pipe ruffles around the cake.

ROSETTES WITH DROP STRINGS A border of rosettes with drop strings gives the cake a lot of dimension. Pipe rosettes with a #18 metal piping tip. Finish the border with drop strings, connecting one rosette to another.

Zigzags with large shells.

Shells with scallops; above is piped "U" embroidery.

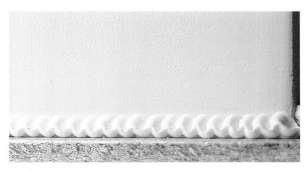

Ruffles.

Rosettes with drop strings.

Piped Flowers in Royal Icing

Before gumpaste flowers became a big hit in America, most cake decorators and designers piped most sugar flowers in royal icing. This was convenient for busy decorators who needed to produce several cakes on any given day or week. Piped from meringue powder royal icing, these flowers can last for months. Use them to adorn cakes iced with royal icing, buttercream, marzipan, or rolled fondant as well as for cupcakes, cookies, brownies, petit fours.

APPLE, ORANGE, CHERRY, AND PEACH BLOSSOMS Apple, orange, cherry, and peach blossoms are made up of five petals; they're all piped the same way. These flowers are lovely and can be produced quickly after you get a handle on manipulating the petal-shaped piping tip and icing nail. With practice, these flowers can be a real time-saver, especially for last-minute cakes.

First, load a pastry bag with a #101 or #102 petal-shaped piping tip and meringue powder royal icing. Next cut up 2x2-inch (5x5-cm) squares of parchment paper. You'll use these squares to pipe the flowers on. The icing can remain white for apple blossoms. Tint the icing delicately with orange, light pink, or peach gel colors for the other blossoms.

Pipe a dot of icing on the flower nail. Put a piece of the parchment square on the dot to secure the paper. Hold the icing nail in your opposite writing hand and the pastry bag in your writing hand. Position the wide end of the piping tip in the center of the icing nail.

Tilt your hands and the piping tip slightly to the right. With steady and even pressure, squeeze the pastry bag and drag the piping tip from the center of the nail, moving up about ½ inch (1.3 cm) and pivoting to the right about ¼ inch (6 mm). Then drag the piping tip back down to the center point where you first began. Both starting and ending position should come to a point. As you squeeze the pastry bag and move the piping tip, slowly rotate the icing nail counterclockwise.

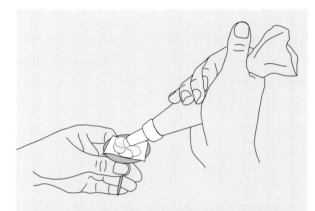

Secure a small square of parchment paper with a dot of icing on an icing nail. Use a #101 or #102 petal-shaped piping tip and load a pastry bag with meringue powder royal icing to pipe the five-petal blossom.

To pipe the next petal, position the piping tip's wide end at the center point, right next to the point of the first petal. Repeat the procedure for the first petal. However, when you pipe the second, third, and fourth petals, the petals should appear next to one another and not overlap. For the last petal, overlap the fifth petal with the

Apple, orange, cherry, and peach blossoms have five petals. Pipe dots of soft yellow icing in the center to finish them.

first petal, raising the tip up slightly as you move back to the center point.

To finish the flower, pipe several dots in the center of the flower with yellow meringue powder royal icing and a #2 round piping tip. Soften the icing with a few drops of water to prevent a take-off point after you pipe the dots.

Use this same technique to pipe all these flowers, whether apple, orange, peach, or cherry blossoms.

VIOLETS Violets can be striking when adorning a cake; they're my favorite piped flower. Pipe many and keep them on hand.

First, load a pastry bag with a #101 or #102 petal-shaped piping tip and meringue powder royal icing that has been colored with violet gel colors. (Make the color a deep shade of violet.) Pipe a dot of icing on the flower nail. Place a piece of the parchment square on the dot to secure the paper. Hold the icing nail in your left hand if you're right-handed and the pastry bag in your right hand. (Reverse these directions if left-handed.) Position the piping tip's wide end in the center of the icing nail.

Use a #101 or #102 petal-shaped tip in a pastry bag loaded with meringue powder royal icing, colored with violet gel colors. Pipe the flower on an icing nail on a small square of parchment paper secured with a dot of icing. When you finish piping the petals, add two points of yellow in the violet's center.

Create a crown of petals for a sumptuous-looking cake. The delicate leaves add to the flowers' realism.

Tilt your hands and the piping tip slightly to the right. With steady and even pressure, squeeze the pastry bag and drag the tip from the center of the nail moving up about ½ inch (1.3 cm) and pivoting to the right about ¼ inch (6 mm). Then drag the tip back down to the center point where you first began. Both the starting and ending positions should come to a point. As you squeeze the pastry bag and move the piping tip, slowly rotate the icing nail counterclockwise.

To pipe the next petal, position the piping tip's wide end at the center point, right next to the point of the first petal. For the second petal, repeat the procedure for creating for the first petal. Now skip a space on the icing nail for the third petal.

The third, fourth, and fifth petals are slightly separate from the first two petals and need to be a little larger. Starting at the flower's center with the piping tip's wide end down, squeeze the pastry bag and move the tip upward about ¾ inch (1.9 cm) and over about ¼ inch (6 mm) and then drag the tip back to the flower's center, coming to a point. Repeat this for the fourth and fifth petal. Remember to ease up a little when bringing the fifth petal to the flower's center.

To finish the violet, pipe two points with yellow royal icing and a #2 metal round piping tip, starting at the center of the flower and dragging the points over the two smaller petals.

PANSIES Pansies are pretty on a variety of iced cakes. They are cheerfully multicolored and come in a variety of shades. To begin, color meringue powder royal icing in two contrasting shades. Place a #102 or #103 metal piping tip in a pastry bag. Add both shades of color in the pastry bag, one shade on the left side and one shade on the right side. Squeeze the bag and let some icing come out. When both colors start to emerge, begin piping the flowers.

Pansies have overlapping petals; pipe them in two contrasting colors. Paint the lines of the pansy using a brush. Pipe a tiny circle of yellow icing in the flower's center.

First, put a dot of icing on the nail and put a piece of parchment on the icing. Position the wide end of the piping tip at the nail's center. Tilt your hands and the tip slightly to the right. With steady and even pressure, squeeze the pastry bag and drag the piping tip from the nail's center, moving up about ½ inch (1.3 cm) and pivoting to the right about ¼ inch (6 mm). Then drag the tip back down to the center point where you first began. Both starting and ending positions should come to a point. As you squeeze the bag and move the tip, slowly rotate the icing nail counterclockwise.

To pipe the next petal, position the wide end of the piping tip at the center point, right next to the first petal's point. Repeat the procedure as you did for the first petal. For the third petal, position the tip back at the flower's center point. Rotate the tip slightly to the left and turn the icing nail slightly clockwise. This will allow you to make the third petal larger. The third and fourth petals overlap the first two petals; they are slightly larger and lower in position than the first two. With heavy pressure, squeeze and move the bag and tip back and forth as you turn the nail counterclockwise. As the third petal overlaps the first petal, drag the tip back to the center point.

For the fourth petal, apply heavy pressure as you squeeze and move the pastry bag and piping tip back and forth as you turn the icing nail counterclockwise. As the fourth petal overlaps the second petal, extend the petal slightly so that the fourth petal is larger than the second petal; then drag the tip back to the center point.

You'll pipe the fifth petal opposite the first four petals. This is the largest petal. Position the piping tip at the end of the fourth petal. Now, with a lot of pressure, squeeze the pastry bag and rotate the piping tip back and forth. Turn the nail as you rotate the tip easing off the pressure as you pull the nail toward the flower's center.

After the flower has dried, paint lines in the center of the flower over the third and fourth petals with violet gel or paste food colors. Pipe a tiny circle with yellow royal icing in the center of the flower.

Note: Remember that pansies come in yellow, pink, lavender, violet, brownish white, and several other color tones and variations.

DAISIES Daisies are cute and timeless. Use a #101 or #102 metal petal-shaped piping tip to pipe daisies. The icing can be white or a daffodil yellow. First, secure a parchment-paper square to the icing nail. This time, you want the small end of the piping tip at the center of the nail. Move the piping tip out about ½ inch (1.3 cm) at 12 o'clock on the clock dial. With steady and even pressure, squeeze the pastry bag, holding the piping tip at a 45° angle. Raise the piping tip barely off the icing nail. Drag the tip to the center of the nail as you ease off the pressure. Turn the nail counterclockwise one-twelfth the distance.

Repeat the procedure and pipe eleven more petals. When piping the last petal, ease the end gently to the flower's center. After these petals dry, finish the flower with dots of yellow icing with a #2 round metal piping tip or one large dot with a #4 round piping tip.

SWEET PEAS Sweet peas can appear as pretty, delicate flowers when gracing cakes. Use a #102 or #103 metal petal-shaped piping tip to pipe these. Sweet peas come in pretty violets or lavenders, pinks, and white.

First, secure a parchment-paper square to the icing nail with a dot of icing on the nail. With the wide end of the petal-shaped piping tip poised at the center of the icing nail, squeeze the pastry bag and turn the nail counterclockwise to form a large back petal. Ease off the pressure on the pastry bag and pull the tip toward the center to end the petal.

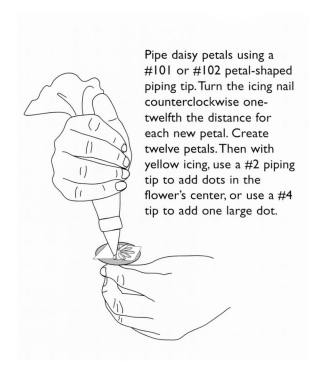

Pipe daisy petals using a #101 or #102 petal-shaped piping tip. Turn the icing nail counterclockwise one-twelfth the distance for each new petal. Create twelve petals. Then with yellow icing, use a #2 piping tip to add dots in the flower's center, or use a #4 tip to add one large dot.

Now, position the piping tip back at the flower's center. Pipe two smaller petals in front of the back petal using the same technique. Now, pipe the flute by positioning the tip at the center of the two smaller petals. Position the wide end of the piping tip at the center point. Squeeze the pastry bag to make a small bud. Pull the tip down to end the bud. Finish the bud with a sepal and calyx with green royal icing.

CHAPTER 7

Gumpaste Sugar Flowers

Nothing looks more natural and beautiful than a sweet arrangement of flowers. We use flowers in many ways in our society to express love, devotion, and sadness as well as to mark celebrations. In the world of cake decorating, flowers adorn and complete iced cakes from the very simple to the elaborately designed. Gumpaste, or sugar, flowers add something to cakes that fresh flowers cannot. They're created painstakingly by hand with petals carefully shaped and dusted, individual flowers wired with stems, and the finished group arranged. Indeed, a gumpaste-flower bouquet is amazing.

Gumpaste is a mixture of confectioners' sugar, corn syrup (or glucose), water, gelatin, egg whites, gum tragacanth (or Tylose), and white vegetable shortening. There are many variations and recipes. (See recipe on p. 141.)

The sugar is elastic and strong and can be rolled petal thin. It can be cut, ruffled, pinched, molded, stretched, and made into many different shapes. Gumpaste is technically edible but not palatable. These sugar ornaments can be removed from the cake and kept for many years as a lovely reminder of the event.

In America, cake designers place gumpaste flowers on cakes iced with buttercream, marzipan, rolled fondant, or royal icing.

WIRES AND GAUGES

Wires and their gauges are important to cake designers. Most flowers made from gumpaste are wired into a spray or arrangement. Some decorators don't wire their flowers. Gumpaste flowers can be mounted on toothpicks or skewers and arranged into the cake.

Most commonly used wire gauges are 28- to 30-gauge for small flowers, and 24- to 26-gauge for larger flowers.

Five-Petal Flowers

Five-petal flowers are perhaps the most useful flowers cake decorators can make. They're the first flowers I learned and the first ones I teach in my beginner gumpaste classes. They have no specific name. Often, we call them filler flowers or pulled blossoms. Because of their size and the ease of making them, these flowers add lightness to an arrangement.

First, take a pea-size amount of gumpaste (white or colored) and place it in the palm of your left hand if you're right-handed. Use the middle finger of your right hand and rotate the paste until you create a small ball. (If you're left-handed use your right palm to hold the gumpaste and shape the ball with your left middle finger.) Now apply light pressure at one end and shape the ball into a small cone.

For the five-petal flower, begin with a pea-size ball of gumpaste. Roll it into a cone shape, and use a modeling stick to open up the cone. Make five small cuts with an X-acto knife in the open cone for petals. With your thumb and forefinger, pull out, shape, and round the petals. Make a small hook in the 28- to 30-gauge wire and insert the small hook into the flower. Shape the trumpet end of the flower on the wire "stem." To complete an arrangement, shape flower buds out of a still smaller ball of gumpaste (far left).

GUMPASTE FIVE-PETAL PULLED FLOWERS

Dip a modeling stick (small sharpened dowel) into a little cornstarch. Insert the stick about ⅛ inch (3 mm) into the head of the cone.

Rotate the stick as you insert it into the cone. Hold the stick in your left hand with the cone on top. (Hold the stick with your right hand if you're left-handed.) With an X-acto knife, cut five evenly spaced slits into the cone. Cut the slits no more than ¼ inch (6 mm) deep.

Open up the slits made from the X-acto knife and hold the end of the cone in your left hand. With your right hand (left hand if you're left-handed) put your index finger under one

of the petals and your thumb on top (or visa versa). Apply light pressure as you press the petal into a smooth shape. Round off the petal with your thumb to take off the square shape. Move on to the next petal and repeat until you have shaped all the petals. Use the modeling stick to make a little opening in the center of the flower.

Take a 28-gauge wire and make a hook at one end. Dip the hook into a little egg white. Ease the unhooked end of the wire into the center of the flower. As you pull the hook inside the flower, rotate the flower. Apply light pressure under the flower with your left hand to shape the trumpet of the flower. Rotate the trumpet with the thumb and middle finger of your right hand, applying pressure at the end of the trumpet. This secures the flower to the wire. (If you're left-handed, reverse hands for these procedures.)

For the bud, begin with a small pea-size gumpaste and roll it into a ball. Insert an unhooked 28-gauge wire into the egg white and ease into the ball. Hold the wire with the bud in your right hand and

take your left hand and pull down on the bottom of the bud, securing it to the wire. If there is moisture on your hands from the egg whites, dip your fingers in a little cornstarch.

To complete the bud, take an X-acto knife and score five lines on the top of the bud. If the bud shrinks because of the pressure of the knife, lightly rotate the middle of the bud to reshape it.

COLOR TIPS

Brush the edge of each petal with a color that contrasts with or is deeper than that of the flower. Add moss green to the flower's center.

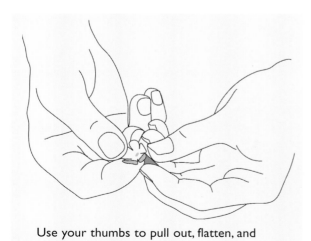

Use your thumbs to pull out, flatten, and shape rounded flower petals.

Four-Petal Flowers

Four-petal pulled blossoms can create lightness in an arrangement. Make them in abundance. Begin with a pea-size amount of white gumpaste and put it in your left hand. Using the middle finger of your right hand, rotate the gumpaste until you create a small ball. (Reverse hands if you're left-handed.) Now apply light pressure at one end and shape the ball into a small cone.

Put a modeling stick (small sharpened dowel) in a little cornstarch. Now insert the  stick about ⅛ inch (3 mm) into the head of the cone. Rotate the stick as you insert it into the cone. Hold the stick in your left hand with the cone on top. Take an X-acto knife and cut four evenly spaced slits into the cone. Cut the slits no more than ¼ inch (6 mm) deep.

Open up the slits made from the X-acto knife and hold the end of the cone in your left  hand. With your right hand, place your index finger under one of the petals and your thumb on top (or visa versa). Apply light pressure as you press the petal into a smooth shape. Now pinch the petal to form a tip at the end of the petal.

Move on to the next petal and repeat until you have shaped all the petals. Take your modeling stick and make a little opening in the flower's center.

Next take a 28-gauge wire and make a hook at one end. Dip the hook into a little egg white. Ease the unhooked end of the wire into the flower. As you pull the hook inside the flower, rotate the flower. Apply light pressure under the flower with your left hand to shape the trumpet of the flower. Rotate the trumpet with your the thumb and middle finger of your right hand, applying pressure at the end of the trumpet. This secures the flower to the wire.

For the bud, begin with a small pea-size bit of gumpaste and roll it into a ball. Insert an unhooked 28-gauge wire into egg white and ease it into the ball. Hold the wire with the bud in your right hand and with your  left hand pinch the top of the bud to a point.

COLOR TIPS

Four-petal pulled flowers resemble the bouvardia, an Australian wildflower. They're white, waxy flowers. Brush egg white on both the flower and bud, or pass them over a steam kettle to form condensation. Let it dry. Brush a little moss green on the back of the flower and bud.

Steps for creating four-petal pulled gumpaste sugar flowers (first four from left). The fifth is the bud, created from a pea-size ball of gumpaste (far right).

GUMPASTE FOUR-PETAL PULLED FLOWERS

Cherry Blossoms

Cherry blossoms help make flower arrangements look pretty and fresh. First, prepare the  stamens for this flower. Because cherry blossoms have many stamens, we can make them from sewing thread. Begin by wrapping white cotton thread around your index and middle fingers. Wrap about 10 times. Attach a hooked 28-gauge wire at each end of the loop. Snip in the middle. Wrap the end of each stamen set with florist tape.

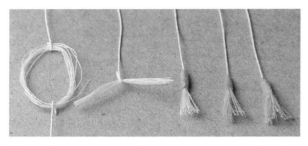

Create flower stamens from several strands of white sewing thread with a hooked 28-gauge wire wrapped with florist tape then dusted with yellow petal dust, dipped in egg white, and dipped into pink petal dust.

Dust the stamens with yellow petal dust. Lightly brush each stamen's tip with a little egg white; then dip it into pinkish petal dust to form pollen.

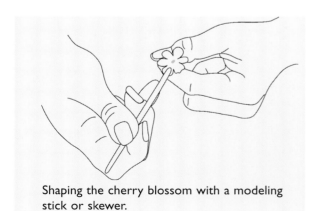

Shaping the cherry blossom with a modeling stick or skewer.

For cherry blossoms, begin with cone-shaped gumpaste. Make five slits, pull out five petals, and open up and soften each petal with a modeling stick. The finished flower has thread stamens. Dust the blossom and stamens separately with petal dust.

For the flower, take a small piece of white or pinkish gumpaste and shape it into a cone. Insert a wooden modeling stick in the head of the paste. Cut five slits with an X-acto knife about ¼ inch (6 mm) deep. Open up the slits and soften each petal with a rounded wooden modeling stick or skewer.

Prepare the skewer by sanding the rough edge with fine sandpaper. Continue to sand until the rough edge becomes round and smooth. Place the flower on the index finger of your left hand. (Use your right hand if you're left-handed.) Make sure there is cornstarch on the index finder. Place the skewer on one of the petals and rotate the stick back and forth to widen the petal. Pull the stick down to shape the petal, making the petal as rounded as possible. Repeat this for each of the petals.

MASTER CHEF'S HINT

Note that the lines in the skewer will appear on each petal, which is characteristic of the flower.

To finish the flower, brush the collected stamens' taped end with egg whites. Insert the wire into the flower. When the taped end of the stamens reach the flower, begin by turning the flower and securing the trumpet of the flower to the wire.

Mimosas

The mimosa is the easiest flower to make and can be the most fun. First, take a pea-size  amount of yellow gumpaste and shape it into a ball. Ease a 28-gauge wire dipped in egg whites into the ball. Make many of these and let them dry for 1 hour.

Brush egg whites on each ball and dip each ball into yellow cornmeal. Let them dry for 1 hour. Gather five to seven mimosa buds and use florist's tape to bind them in a spray.

To make the mimosa, begin with a pea-size ball of yellow gumpaste. Insert a wire. Let dry, brush with egg white and dip into yellow cornmeal. Collect five to seven and tape them into a spray.

Roses

Roses have timeless beauty, and they're among nearly everyone's favorite flowers. Creating gumpaste roses requires many steps. First, determine the size of rose you would like to make. Rose petal cutters vary in shapes and sizes. For a medium to large rose, choose  the third cutter in the petal series. Use this cutter to estimate your rose base. The height of the rose base is more important than the base's width.

Next take a ball of gumpaste and shape it into a cone. Measure the cone to see if it fits the height of the petal cutter you're starting with. Ease a 24-gauge hooked wire into the

The cone-shaped base for your rose should fit into one of these patterns, depending on the size of rose desired.

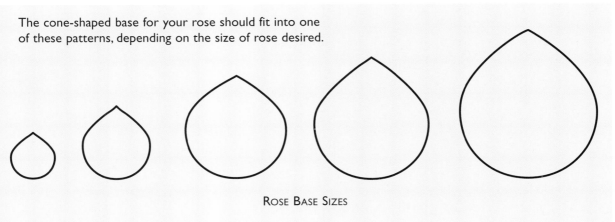

ROSE BASE SIZES

To make the gumpaste sugar rose, begin with a ball of gumpaste and shape it into a cone. Make a small hook in a 24-gauge wire and insert it into the cone shape. Cut the first petal out of rolled gumpaste, soften its edges with a dogbone tool, and carefully wrap it around the middle of the cone. Brush it lightly with egg white, and place a second petal over the seam, slightly higher than the first petal. Continue attaching petals, overlapping them about one-third. The third petal will go inside the fourth petal, and so on.

base of the cone. Insert the wire about ½ inch (1.25 cm) and slightly pull back on the wire to engage the hook. Pull down on the gumpaste to seal the paste to the wire. Make several bases and let them dry for 24 hours.

Rub a little white vegetable shortening on your work area. Roll out a piece of gumpaste on the shortening. Roll the paste until you can see through the paste. Carefully pick up the paste and put it on a surface lightly sprinkled with cornstarch. Cut four petals with the medium-size cutter. Put the pieces on a cell pad and lightly soften the edges with a ball or dog-bone tool. Place the petals under plastic wrap to prevent them from drying.

Pick up the rose base and lightly brush it with egg whites. Pick up one of the petals in your left hand and the wired base in your right hand. (If you're left-handed, reverse hands.) Bring the tip of the base one-third the distance from the top of the petal. Press the petal to the base. Tuck the left side of the petal to the base and overlap the right side of the petal, leaving a tiny opening at the top of the petal. Slightly pull the right side back with your thumb for a pretty detail.

Brush the first petal and base lightly with egg whites. Take the second petal and place it over the seam, slightly higher than the first petal. If you're right-handed, brush the right side of the second petal (about one-third the distance of the petal). Attach the third petal to the egg-wash side, overlapping about one-third back. Brush the third petal with egg white (one-third the distance). Attach the fourth petal to the egg-wash side. The right side of the fourth petal should go inside the second petal. Brush egg white on the fourth petal and overlap the second petal inside the fourth petal.

Slightly open up the petals and pinch the center of each petal for nice detailing. (If you're left-handed, you would want to brush the left side of the second petal and continue to arrange your petals that way.)

Next cut five more petals with the same medium-size cutter. Soften the edge of each petal as you did for the previous four petals. Attach the fifth petal to the seam of any one of the overlapped petals. This petal should be slightly higher than the others. Egg wash and overlap each petal. Once attached, pinch the center of each petal for detailing. Let this dry for 24 hours.

Next measure the flower to see if the fourth cutter covers it from top to base; if not, use the fifth cutter. Cut five more petals. Use a ball tool on each petal to soften the edges. Let these petals dry slightly before attaching them (because of their size). With egg whites, lightly brush the rose base with its nine petals. Attach

each petal as you did the last five. They should be slightly higher than the previous petals. Because of the size of these petals, you may have to turn the rose upside down to dry. Let it dry about 15 to 20 minutes; then turn it right side up and pinch the petals for a final finish.

To complete the rose, roll out a piece of mint green gumpaste. Cut out the calyx with a medium-size calyx cutter. Ease the calyx on the wire first. Then brush each sepal with egg whites. Ease it onto the back of the rose. Put a small pea-size green paste on back of the calyx and shape it on the wire to complete the rose.

COLOR TIPS

Brush the rose's center with a deeper color. Then take the deep shade and, starting at the outside, brush the inside edge of each petal. For a richer effect, brush the very edge of each petal with a contrasting color.

Rose Leaves

Rose leaves can be used to complete many arrangements. Roll a piece of green gumpaste into a sausage shape. Then roll one end of the sausage, leaving a ridge at one end and making it petal thin at the other end.

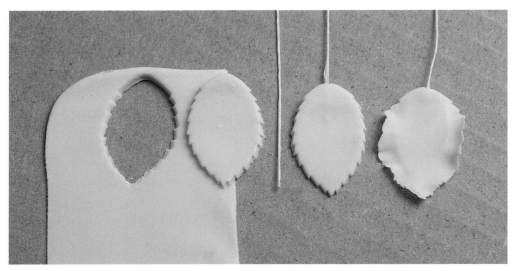

Use a rose-leaf cutter to cut out the rose leaf from mint green gumpaste. Ease in a 28-gauge wire, and use a ball tool around the leaf's edges to give the leaf a more natural look.

Position the back of the rose-leaf cutter at the ridge. Cut as many petals as you can. Dip the end of a 28-gauge wire (without a hook) into egg whites. Ease the wire tip about ¼ inch (6 mm) inside the petal's wide end. Pinch to secure to the wire. Repeat this for all the other rose leaves.

For a leaf impression, press the back of a real rose leaf to the gumpaste petal for veins, or use a rose-leaf press. Soften the edge of each of the rose leaves with a ball or dogbone tool.

COLOR TIPS

For rose leaves, use moss-green petal dust with a little cornstarch to soften the color. Brush the color in a circular motion on the front of the leaf, being careful not to go to the leaf's edge. Do the same for the back of the leaf.

Now brush moss green (full strength) up the leaf's center. Use pink or yellow petal dust to brush a little color at its broad upper left corner to create a a sunlit effect. Finally, brush the very edge of the leaf with full-strength moss green.

Carnations

Carnations are a welcome treat for cake designers. The secret is to use a rounded toothpick  for ruffling the petals. First, make a base for the carnation. Take a tiny piece of gumpaste and roll it into a ball. Dip a 24-gauge wire into egg whites and insert the wire into the ball. Take your thumb and middle finger and rotate the paste, applying pressure at the end of the paste to secure it to the wire. The "bud" should look like a Q-tip and be no longer than ½ inch (1.25 cm).

Next choose a carnation cutter or a small scalloped cookie cutter. Cookie cutters are my favorite tools for making carnations because the scallops are small. Roll out a piece of white or pastel-colored gumpaste on vegetable shortening. Roll it very thin. Transfer paste onto the cornstarch. Cut out three petals with a small scalloped cookie cutter. Cover the petals with plastic wrap. Put one of the petals on a little cornstarch and cut little slits in each of the scallops (about ¼ inch or 6 mm deep).

Take a rounded toothpick and place about ½ inch (1.25 cm) of the toothpick on the petal. Use your index or middle finger to rotate the toothpick back and forth to ruffle the petals. Continue to do this on each of the scallops.

Ruffle the other two petals and place them under plastic to keep moist. Brush the carnation base with a little egg white. Ease the wire through the center of one of the petals.

Roll a rounded toothpick back and forth on the scallops of the carnation petals to create ruffles.

Sandwich the base in the center of the petal.

Brush egg white up the petal's center and overlap the left side. Put a little egg white on the overlapped side. Overlap the right side of the petal. Gently gather the petal, applying light pressure at the trumpet of the flower while carefully shaping the flower. This is the first floret.

Brush egg whites on the first floret. Ease the second petal on the floret as you did the first. Sandwich the floret and overlap the petal. Gently gather the petal to make the florets fuller. Repeat this with the third petal. However, reverse the side of the petal so that the ruffles are on the underside. Egg wash, sandwich, and overlap the petal. Gently gather until the ruffles explode in frilliness.

For the calyx, roll a ball of gumpaste and shape it into a cone. Put the modeling stick in cornstarch and insert it inside the wide end of the cone. Roll the modeling stick with the paste onto the work surface and widen the interior of the paste. Reverse the wide end and place

Make a Q-tip-style base with gumpaste and unhooked wire. Roll out gumpaste and use a small scalloped cutter to cut out petals. Cut tiny slits in each scallop and use a rounded toothpick to ruffle each scallop. Ease the wire through the petal's center that's brushed with egg white. Gather and shape the petal, applying light pressure at the flower's trumpet.

GUMPASTE CARNATIONS

on it on the work surface, making a Mexican hat. Pinch the brim making it smaller. Roll a rounded toothpick on the wide part of the hat, making it as thin as possible. Place a small rose calyx cutter over the brim and cut out the calyx. Insert a modeling stick into the cavity. Widen the cavity by pressing each of the sepals (modified leaves comprising the calyx) against the modeling stick.

To complete the flower, ease the carnation into the calyx. Brush the interior of the calyx with egg whites. Place the carnation trumpet inside the calyx. At the end of the calyx, use a rounded toothpick and move up ¼ inch (6 mm). Apply pressure as you turn the wire, creating a little bud under the calyx. Pinch the end of the bud to secure it to the wire.

COLOR TIPS

Brush the carnation's center with a deep color. Carefully wipe the same color over each ruffle.

MAKING THE CARNATION'S TRUMPET

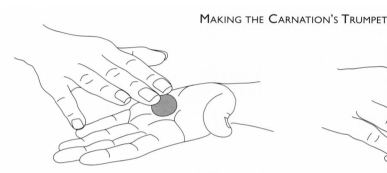

1. For the flower's trumpet, begin with a ball of mint green gumpaste.

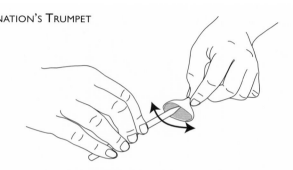

3. Continue modeling the opening, beginning to create a Mexican hat shape.

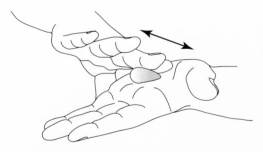

2. Roll the gumpaste into a cone shape.

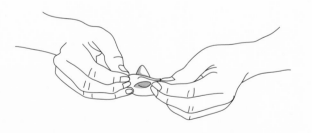

4. Create a brim for the Mexican hat shape.

3. Insert a modeling stick into the center of the wide end of the cone, opening it up.

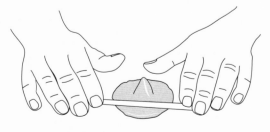

5. Flatten the brim by rolling it out with the modeling stick. Maintain the peak in the Mexican hat shape.

Cymbidium Orchids

Cymbidium orchids are breathtakingly beautiful flowers. To make them, each sepal (you may  call them "petals" instead of sepals) is separately wired to create a realistic look. To begin, color gumpaste in yellow, moss green, pink, or natural white. For colored paste, use a small piece of gumpaste and add white to it. This paste will be for the orchid's "lip."

Next roll a ball of gumpaste into a long sausage shape. Dip a 26- or 24-gauge wire into egg whites (about ½ inch or 1.25 cm deep). Insert the wire into the gumpaste about ½ to 1 inch (1.25 to 2.5 cm) deep. Press a modeling stick on the center of the wired gumpaste. Then thin each side of the wired paste, leaving a ridge in the center. Make sure vegetable shortening is on the work surface when thinning the sides.

Pick up the wired gumpaste and turn the paste so that it's facing you with the wire at 12 o'clock. Put the gumpaste back on the shortening. Cut a freehand oval shape for one of the sepals. Or pick up the wired paste and place it on a little cornstarch. Cut the sepal with an oval-shaped petal cutter. Emboss the petal with a cornhusk veiner (to form lines) and lightly soften the edge of the sepal.

GUMPASTE CYMBIDIUM ORCHIDS

Each gumpaste sepal or petal is created from rolled gumpaste that is wired and cut out with an oval or other shape of petal cutter. The finished petals are assembled with the aid of the wires into an orchid.

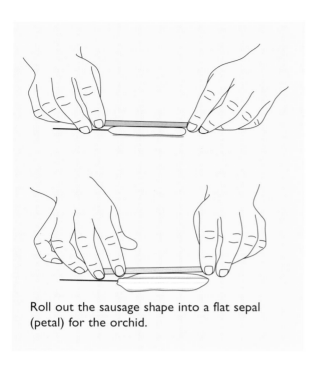

Roll out the sausage shape into a flat sepal (petal) for the orchid.

ing a ridge in the center. Place the wired paste on a little cornstarch and cut it with a lip cutter. Emboss with cornhusk to form lines. Lightly soften the edge of the lip. Then ruffle the three scallops (only) in front of the lip with a rounded toothpick. Carefully bend the lip backwards and raise up the two back scallops, pinching it toward the center of the lip. Let it dry over a large rolling pin.

While the lip is drying, complete the back of the lip by rolling a pea-size piece of gumpaste into a small sausage shape and pull the ends together to form an upside-down "U." Brush the back of the drying lip with a little egg white. Attach the gumpaste.

Make the column of the flower by shaping a small ball of gumpaste into a cone shape. Ease a 26- or 24-gauge wire, dipped in egg whites and into the cone's narrow part. Hollow out the cone shape with a ball tool, leaving a ridge at the top of the column. Attach a tiny ball of paste at the center top of the column with a little egg white. Let dry for 2 hours.

Then shape the sepals over a large rolling pin and let dry. Repeat this four more times for a total of five petals.

Roll another sausage piece of gumpaste and wire the paste. Thin each side of the paste, leav-

ASSEMBLING THE CYMBIDIUM ORCHID

Assemble the Cymbidium orchid sepals (petals), beginning with the innermost sepals and working outward.

Gumpaste sugar flowers (from the left) rose bud, rose leaf, rose, azalea, pulled five-petal flower and bud, carnation, Cymbidium orchid, cherry blossoms, and mimosa. Petal dust helps make the flowers look realistic. Carefully brush on petal dust, using a deep shade in the flower's center and on the edges of petals. Use a lighter shade for the rest of the petal. Adding color to gumpaste flowers is an art, as you'll soon realize.

Complete the lip by attaching the column to the back of the lip and tape securely with florist's tape.

To assemble the flower, tape the sepals to each side of the lip. This forms the "legs." Then tape two more sepals above the legs to form the "arms." Last, tape the "head" to the orchid, facing inward or outward to the other taped sepals. Finish this dramatic flower with petal dust.

COLOR TIPS

Petal dust each sepal in a deeper shade of the chosen color. Brush the color up the sepal's center, leaving the sepal's edges neutral. Then use the deeper shade to brush on the very edge of each sepal. Brush a little moss green at the base of each sepal.

For the "lip," use petal dust in a deeper shade. Brush burgundy-colored petal dust on the ruffled area of the lip and above the ruffle. Then paint the ruffled edge with burgundy paste or gel color to create depth. Also paint little dots on the lip with burgundy paste color.

Brush the upside-down "U" shape with egg whites and sprinkle a little yellow cornmeal for pollen. Brush the center of the column with egg white and add cornmeal for pollen. Add some dots of burgundy to the column's center.

To make the azalea, begin with a large ball of gumpaste; shape it into a cone. Using a modeling stick, open up the center of the cone and create a Mexican hat shape with a broad brim. With a five-petal cutter, cut petals out of the brim. Soften each petal with a ball or dogbone tool. Gather six plastic stamens, fold to make twelve, and secure them with florist's tape on a hooked 24-gauge wire. Insert the stamens and wire into the flower. Brush the flower deep inside with petal dust. Add dots of color with a toothpick.

Azaleas

Azaleas can be fashioned quickly and made in abundance and wired or arranged into a spray.

First, prepare the stamens. For this flower, you'll need to use plastic stamens; sewing thread is too weak for 11 stamens. Take 6 stamens and secure them on a hooked 24-gauge wire. When folded, you'll have 12 stamens. Cut one of the stamens or leave it. Tape the stamens securely with florist's tape.

Use a large piece of gumpaste and shape it into a cone. Dip a modeling stick into cornstarch and insert it into the head of the cone. Apply pressure as you roll the gumpaste to open up the paste to form a shape like a little Mexican hat.

See drawings for five steps for making a Mexican hat shape out of gumpaste on p. 86. Instead of ruffling the petals as you would for the carnation, use a five-petal azalea cutter to cut out the five petals.

After you cut out the shape with an azalea cutter, press each of the flower's petals on cornhusk to form lines and carefully soften the edge of each petal with a ball tool. Brush egg white on the florist's tape of the stamens and insert wire through the azalea's center. Apply pressure to secure the trumpet of the flower to the wire.

COLOR TIPS

Lightly brush the azalea's center with light burgundy petal dust. Carefully add burgundy dots (with a toothpick) on one or two of the petals deep inside the flower.

Flower Arranging

Arrange gumpaste flowers in a ball of rolled fondant or tape them into a spray with florist's tape. A taped floral spray can also be arranged in rolled fondant. Cut the flowers and arrange them in a circle. Position the larger flowers first. Place leaves in between the large flowers with smaller blossoms appearing on top of the leaves. Use more leaves toward the center of the arrangement and lots of small blossoms and medium-size flowers to fill up the arrangement. Cut the wires, leaving 1 to 1½ inches (2.5 to 3.8 cm) of wire to be inserted into the fondant. No two flowers should be on the same level.

Use a ball of rolled fondant for arranging flowers. Push the wire stems into the rolled fondant ball. Or gather and arrange the flowers into a spray and use florist's tape to secure them. For the most pleasing arrangement, have no two flowers at the same level.

Original photo by Jeff Harris, slanted for *Bride's* magazine, fall 1998

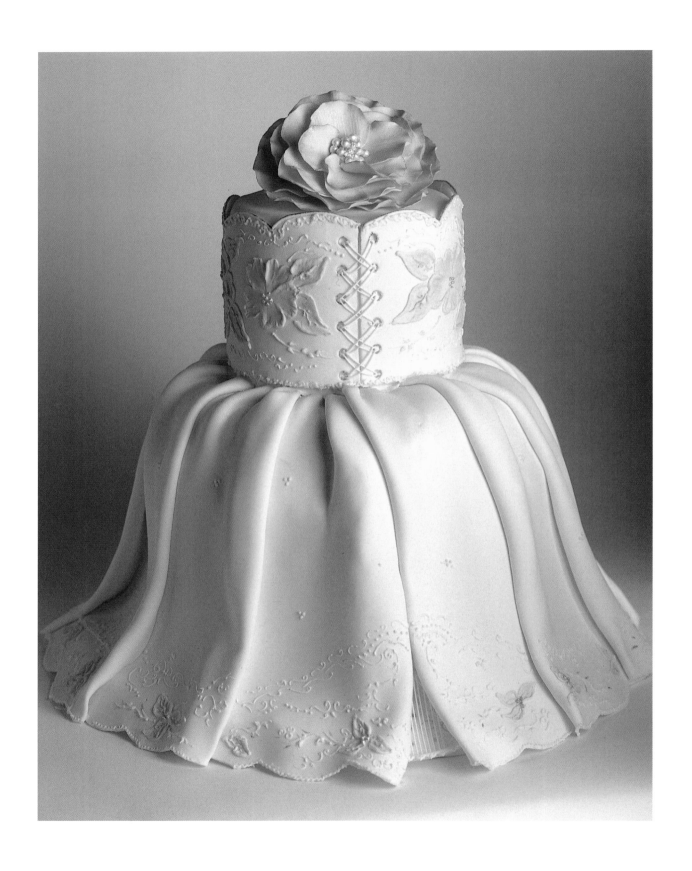

CHAPTER 8

Ornaments, Inscriptions, Drapery & Toppers

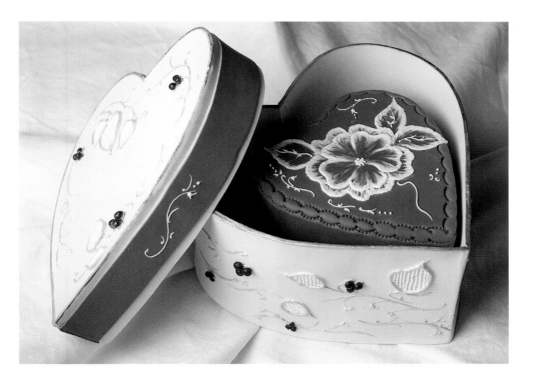

What's on top of the cake can make even an otherwise ordinary cake into something spectacular. The top ornament is usually the focal point of the cake's design. On top of the cake we can arrange a beautiful spray of gumpaste flowers, use fresh flowers, pipe a monogram or a message in calligraphy, pile blown-sugar balls, decorate with bells or other shapes, celebrate with bride and groom mice, show off sugar or fabric ribbons, add elegant drapery, or use brush painting. We'll also show you how to use lovely cameos, create swans or other birds, or fashion heart-shaped boxes.

With so many elegant finishing touches to choose from, your creative expression will grow in leaps and bounds after you master the various arts of gracing a cake with more than a simple icing or a lovely buttercream rose.

Writing Inscriptions

Writing inscriptions can be one of the most difficult things to do because it's usually the final touch after you've spent hours carefully decorating the cake. Even seasoned cake designers may feel a little clumsy or fear that they will mess up the cake if they write on it. Here are a few tricks for writing inscriptions without disturbing an elegant design and a few ways to correct mistakes.

Writing on sugar plaques made from gumpaste, pastillage, marzipan, modeling chocolate, or rolled fondant allow more freedom than writing directly on the iced cake or writing on buttercream. If you make a mistake or you don't like the way something is written, just scratch the message out with a toothpick and rewrite it. After they're inscribed, these plaques can be placed on an iced cake, removed before serving, and saved as a keepsake or eaten with the cake if they're made from marzipan, modeling chocolate, or rolled fondant.

Corner bakeries tend to use handwritten script or printed block letters commonly with the popular greeting, "Happy Birthday." Practice lettering using royal icing, piping gel, or melted chocolate with a little oil or corn syrup added. It's best to practice with a small paper cone because the cone will give you more control when lettering. Decorating your writing with piped, drop, or plunger flowers can enhance the design and distract viewers from any imperfect lettering.

One way to achieve good writing skills is to trace a beautiful print or script. Photocopy to enlarge your example. Put tracing paper (make sure that you can see through it) over the example and tape the corners down on your lettering sample with masking tape. Then trace the lettering using a small paper cone. If the lettering is large, you can put a #2 or #3 round metal piping tip in the paper cone. If the writing is script or calligraphy, put a #0 or #1 metal round piping tip in the paper cone or pipe without a piping tip. Do this exercise many times. Then do the exercise without using the pattern beneath the tracing paper. The more you practice, the better you'll become.

Use many techniques in your writing skills. Flood the initial letter of the greeting for a dramatic effect. Or flood and then satin stitch the letter for a beautifully textured look. You can also trace traditional calligraphy or monogrammed alphabets from many books and then transfer the designs onto a sugar plaque.

If you write your inscriptions on sugar plaques, you won't have to worry about ruining a perfectly iced cake. Just scratch out mistakes with a toothpick.

The more you practice, the better you will become and the more comfortable you'll feel when writing.

When piping in script or calligraphy, slightly drag the metal piping tip to the surface as you pipe. Pipe at a 45° angle. The lines of the letters should overlap as though you were writing in cursive style. Your upstrokes should have a fine line and your down strokes should have a heavier line.

When piping block or print lettering, use the lift and drop techniques, especially when piping straight lines or curves. When the lines and curves are extremely short or small, the piping tip should be slightly above the surface, almost as though you were tracing the letters.

For creating monograms, we've provided lettering sample alphabets on pp. 162–169 that you can use. Either trace or photocopy the chosen letter(s) and place it under a sheet of plastic wrap secured over the photocopy. Begin to outline and flood the monogram initials in royal icing. Air dry the monogram before placing it on a rolled iced cake or plaque.

This inscription uses a simple block letter for an initial capital that has been outlined, flooded, and overpiped. The other letters were piped freehand, then overpiped in another color. Violets were piped in royal icing. Floral flourishes and lacy scrolls complete the design.

These initials have letters outlined and flooded in royal icing. The raised letters are then given more dimension and texture with satin-stitch embroidery.

Sugar Ribbon Bouquets

Sugar ribbon bouquets create easy and beautiful ornaments on cakes that you can make weeks or months in advance before assembly. You'll need about seventy pieces to create a bouquet.

First, take white or any colored gumpaste and roll it thin. Square off the paste using a ruler and X-acto knife. Cut and carefully measure strips of paste about 3½ to 4 inches (8.9 to 10 cm) long and ½ inch (1.3 cm) wide. Cover strips with plastic wrap to prevent drying.

Next shape 26- or 24-gauge white wires in an upside down "U" shape. Brush the top and bottom of each sugar strip with egg white. Put the shaped wire about ¼ inch from the strip's

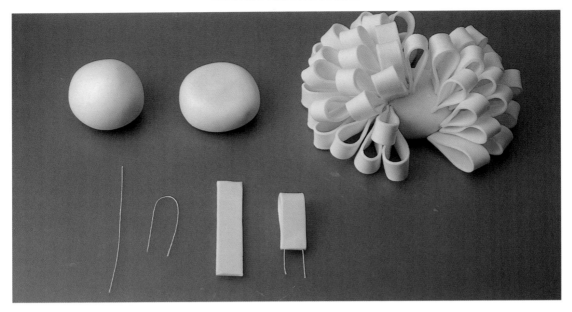

To make a ribbon bouquet, begin with a ball of gumpaste. Roll the gumpaste thin. Use a ruler and an X-acto knife to carefully cut and measure strips ½ inch (1.3 cm) wide and 3½ to 4 inches (7.5 to 10 cm) long. Shape white wires in an upside-down "U" shape. Insert the "U" into the gumpaste ribbon strip about ¼ inch (0.75 cm) deep. Then bend the strip over into a closed "U" shape. Insert the wired ribbons into a large round ball of gumpaste. Continue to add small ribbon strips to create a large ribbon bouquet.

bottom. Close the top strip on the bottom strip, sandwiching the wire. Turn the ribbon strip standing-side up and let it dry. Repeat this for sixty-nine more ribbon strips.

When ready to assemble, shape a large ball of rolled fondant into a disk about 2½ inches (6.4 cm) in diameter. Snip the ribbon wires so that they're no more than ½ inch (1.3 cm) long. Insert the flat or standing sides of the wired ribbon loops into the ball of rolled fondant.

Bells

Nothing seems to evoke the thought of weddings or anniversaries more than bells or bell shapes. Gumpaste bells can adorn an iced cake or be given out as wedding favors.

To mold them, take a large amount of gumpaste and massage a little white vegetable shortening into the gumpaste to make it more pliable. Dust the bell mold with cornstarch. Press the gumpaste into the mold and, using your thumbs, shape the paste against the mold. Immediately remove the gumpaste from the mold to prevent sticking. Dust the mold with cornstarch again and place the molded paste back into the mold. Press and shape again. Release the molded gumpaste again to check for sticking.

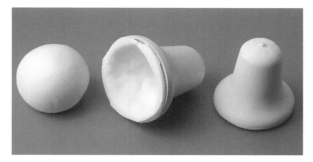

Use softened gumpaste and a bell mold to create a gumpaste sugar bell. Cornstarch inside the mold will help you release a perfect bell after the gumpaste dries in 2 to 4 hours inside the mold.

Replace the molded paste back into the mold and shape once more. Cut away any excess from the bottom of the mold. Let the paste dry in the mold for 2 to 4 hours.

Release the molded paste and let it dry an additional 24 hours. When completely dried, lightly sand the edges. Decorate with plunger flowers, royal iced flowers, embroidery piping, "C" scrolls, gilded monograms, and pyramid piping. You can also create a beautiful brush painting with gel food colors.

MASTER CHEF'S HINT

For shaping bells, try white modeling chocolate or commercial rolled fondant instead of gumpaste.

This bell, molded from gumpaste, was adorned with brush painting.

Brush Painting

Brush painting allows you to quickly decorate a cake, plaque, bell, or any hard surface. Use a round brush or a Chinese brush, first practicing basic strokes on plain paper. Your brush strokes should move freely with light pressure. To give the strokes dimension, use light and dark gel food colors in contrasting shades.

First, create your palate by using gel or paste colors. To create pastels, add liquid whitener to some of the colors. Dip your brush in a little water to make the colors more fluid. Begin with a stroke that has a slight curve. Use heavier pressure when you start; then ease up, using lighter pressure when you end the stroke. After you've finished your basic stroke, outline it with a darker shade for contrast.

For flowers, dip the brush in pinks, yellows, violets, or liquid whitener and paint a circle of five dots for flowers. Pull out stems from the flowers for a more realistic look.

For brush painting, use food color gels and a round or Chinese brush. Practice on plain paper, moving freely with light pressure. Create your palate of colors, adding liquid whitener to some colors. Dip your brush in a little water to make the colors more fluid. Use heavier pressure when beginning a stroke and lighter pressure finishing the stroke. Outline in darker color for contrast. Dots can suggest flower petals.

Bride & Groom Mice

This adorable couple, bride and groom mice, are so cute you could eat them. Making little mice from the body to the clothing is great fun. Your guests will admire them.

First, make some brown, beige, or gray gumpaste for the body. Use the mouse parts patterns on p. 99 to size the height and shape of the body, head, ears, and arms.

MOUSE BODY   Shape a round piece of gumpaste into a cone with a dull or flat top.

MOUSE HEAD AND EARS   Shape a small piece of gumpaste into a cone with a soft point. With a small ball tool, indent the left and right side of the cone for the ear sockets. Roll a tiny piece of gumpaste into a ball. Use a small ball tool and press the center of the paste on a cell pad. Pull it toward you to form an ear. Put a dot of egg white in each ear socket and gently place the ears in the sockets on the head.

MOUSE ARMS   Shape a small piece of gumpaste into a little sausage. Use a ball tool to press each end of the gumpaste sausage shape. Pull the tool toward you on a cell pad to form the palms of the hands. Cut five slits into each palm with an X-acto knife to form fingers.

MOUSE BRIDE   For the mouse bride's clothing, roll out a piece of white gumpaste on vegetable shortening. Cut out two scalloped pieces on cornstarch for the dress and petticoat and one or two small scalloped pieces for the pinafore. Ruffle the pieces on a little cornstarch with a rounded toothpick.

Dab a little egg white on top of the mouse bride's body. Drape the petticoat over the little gumpaste body. Fluff up the petticoat with a dry paintbrush. Dot a little egg white on the top center of the petticoat. Add the dress. Fluff up the dress with a dry paintbrush. Dot a little egg white on the center top of the dress. Put the mouse bride's arms over the dress and pull them together because the she will be holding a spray of flowers.

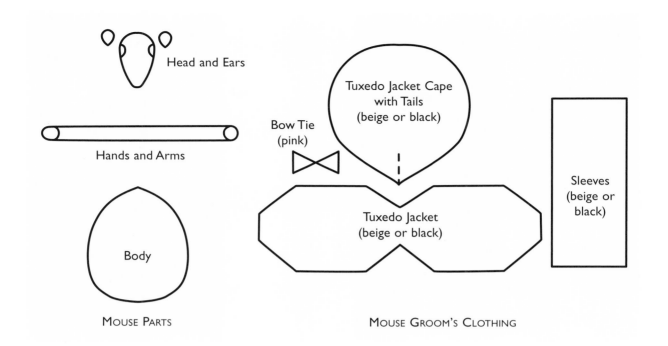

Head and Ears

Hands and Arms

Body

MOUSE PARTS

Bow Tie
(pink)

Tuxedo Jacket Cape
with Tails
(beige or black)

Tuxedo Jacket
(beige or black)

Sleeves
(beige or
black)

MOUSE GROOM'S CLOTHING

Create the mouse body from a ball of gumpaste formed into the pattern shape. Create a cone shape for the head, cut out little mouse ears and attach them to the head, and form the arms and hands from a sausage roll of gumpaste. Assemble the mouse bride following the steps in the second row below and the mouse groom following the steps in the bottom row below. Use white gumpaste for the bride's dress and beige or black gumpaste for the groom's tuxedo.

MOUSE BRIDE AND GROOM ASSEMBLY

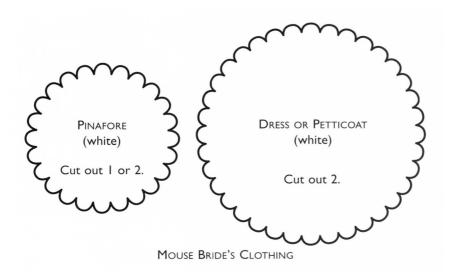

PINAFORE
(white)

Cut out 1 or 2.

DRESS OR PETTICOAT
(white)

Cut out 2.

MOUSE BRIDE'S CLOTHING

MOUSE GROOM For the mouse groom's clothing, roll out a piece of dark brown or black gumpaste to create the vest, cape, sleeves, and bow tie. With a little egg white, attach the vest to the body with the ends of the vest toward the back of the body.

Brush the sleeves with egg whites. Roll up the arms in the sleeves. Form the palms of the hands by pressing a ball tool at each end of the sleeve. Cut slits for fingers.

Dot a little egg white on the top of the body and attach the arms. Let the arms hang by the sides of the body. Cut a small slit at the end of the cape for tuxedo tails. Dot a little egg white on the arms to attach the cape. On the top of the cape, use another dot of egg white to attach the head in the center. On the body just beneath the head, dot egg white to attach the bow tie.

For the mouse groom's boutonniere, make a miniature plunger flower for him to wear over the heart. (See chapter 7.)

Dot a little egg white on the arms. Put one or two of the pinafores over the arms, which will hide most of the arms. Dot egg white on the top of the pinafore. Position the head in the center. Make small miniature plunger flowers to be held in the center of her hands and glued with royal icing. Pipe a Cornelli lace design on top of her head for a lacey bridal veil, or pipe the design on plastic wrap, let air dry, and attach the veil to her head with a dot of royal icing.

Note: The mouse bride's arms can be covered with white sleeves that are attached to the dress. However, most of her arms will be covered by the pinafore.

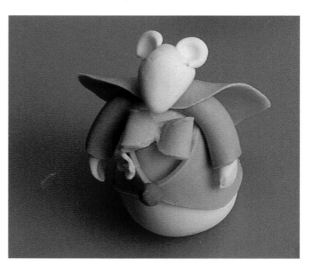

Blown Sugar Balls

Blown sugar balls are spectacular; they appear like crystal balls or orbits of light. They make stunning ornaments that are not often seen atop a wedding cake. Blown sugar balls are a beautiful and unusual alternative to sugar flowers. Making them requires several pieces of equipment, quickness, and getting used to working with extremely hot sugar. Be careful that you don't burn yourself.

For consistent success in blowing and pulling sugar, work with Isomalt sugar instead of regular granulated or superfine sugar. Granulated and superfine sugar may contain impurities that will turn the sugar yellow. Weather can also drastically affect the consistency of the sugar, making it necessary to constantly adjust the amount of tartaric acid in the recipe. Isomalt is complete and requires no acid. The pot and utensils used in cooking the sugar must be in pristine condition.

Made from sucrose, Isomalt is white, crystalline, and odorless. It is a mixture of two disaccharide alcohols: gluco-mannitol and gluco-sorbitol. Isomalt cooks in half the time it takes to cook sugar in the traditional way. When it melts, it will be absolutely clear which will allow you to create clear blown balls. You can also color Isomalt sugar.

There's a laundry list of equipment needed for a wide range of sugar applications. However, to make blown balls, you'll need to have a silicone baking sheet (silpat), a marble slab, a high-intensity lamp, one or two blowing sticks with a pump, a spirit burner with denatured alcohol, latex gloves, a set of metal bars for containing the syrup while it cools, a mercury or good candy thermometer, a hair dryer (that blows cold air), a microwave, and a large closed container with plenty of desiccant. (To find Isomalt distributors and other suppliers, see Special Cake-Decorating Supplies on pp. 170–171.)

First, make the Isomalt sugar according to the recipe and carefully follow directions. Before pouring the Isomalt onto a silpat to cool, cast any pieces you may need later to assemble your sugar pieces. (See "Casting" on p. 102.) Then pour the remaining Isomalt sugar directly on a silpat or inside an enclosed area that you create with the metal bars.

Equipment for blown sugar balls. You'll also need latex gloves to handle the sugar, but they won't protect you from the heat or from burns. Be certain that the hot sugar cools before handling it. Take great care because hot sugar can cause serious burns.

BLOWING STICK AND PUMP FOR BLOWN SUGAR BALLS

½ to ¾ inch (1.3 to 1.9 cm) above the blowing stick to separate the ball shape from the stick. This area will be heated over a spirit burner when you cut the ball away from the stick.

Continue to pump air and rub the top of the sugar with your hands to cool it. Hold the pump alternately right side up and upside down while you continue to slowly pump air to maintain the round shape of the ball. After the ball is the desired size, blow the ball cold with the hair dryer. This will also help maintain its shape. Once cold, heat the area above the blowing stick over the spirit burner. When the sugar softens, carefully cut it with a pair of scissors. Put the dried ball in the closed container with desiccant. The desiccant is used to keep moisture away from the sugar. Repeat this many more times until you have enough sugar balls for your project.

Put on the latex gloves. Let the sugar cool before handling it. If you aren't using metal bars, use the outside edge of the silpat to contain the Isomalt sugar in the center. As the sugar cools, pick up the sugar and move it to another area on the silpat. Do this several times. Since we aren't pulling the sugar to make flowers and foliage, we can let the sugar sit and set up. When it's cool enough to handle, cut the sugar into several pieces. Put two to three pieces of Isomalt sugar under a high-intensity lamp to keep the sugar soft. The latex gloves protect the sugar, keeping it shiny. They don't, however, protect you from the heat or make the sugar less hot. When sufficiently soft, fold one piece of Isomalt sugar several times. Cut a piece that's about the size of a golf ball. Make a cavity in the center of the sugar. Warm one of the blowing sticks attached to a pump over the spirit burner. Put the stick inside the sugar cavity and seal it in the sugar.

Squeeze the pump several times until the sugar begins to expand. Carefully rub the top of the sugar lightly to cool it. Pump a little more air into the sugar to expand it some more. Carefully pull the sugar, extending the ball of sugar

CASTING To assemble the balls into a top ornament, cast a rounded disk by pouring some of the cooked sugar into a large rounded metal cutter that has been lightly oiled with corn oil. Put a piece of aluminum foil under the cutter on a silpat. Pour the hot sugar into the cutter and fill up the area of the cutter to ⅛ to ¼ inch (3 to 6 mm) high. Let the sugar cool and harden. This could take 30 minutes to 1 hour. When cooled, carefully remove the hard sugar from the metal cutter. You have just cast your first piece.

Take out the blown balls and assemble the them, using a piece of the Isomalt sugar softened with the spirit burner. The melting Isomalt will glue the blown balls together.

Cameos & Wooden Molds

Cameos and ornamental molds are easy to make and are beautiful on the sides of medium to large cakes or on the top of a smaller cake. If you can allow them sufficient time to dry, you can make them out of rolled fondant.

Take a medium to large piece of rolled fondant or gumpaste and roll it into a ball with a little vegetable shortening. Rub a little vegetable shortening in the cavity of the wooden or plastic mold. Press the ball of paste into the cavity. Turn the mold over and apply pressure. Release the paste from the mold. Allow the paste to dry for one hour and carefully trim away the excess. Let dry completely for 24 hours. If the molds are to be used on the sides of the cake, then dry the paste on a curved surface.

Heart Box

This heart box can be made from gumpaste or pastillage. Gumpaste will allow you more time to add the curved pieces around the heart's base. Pastillage will give you a very limited time. For a small box, try gumpaste. However, for a large box or other large three-dimensional structures, it's best to use pastillage.

First, cut out two heart shapes, one a little larger than the other. (See the Heart Pattern on p. 104.) The hearts should be no thicker than ⅛ inch (3 mm). The larger heart will be the lid. Let the hearts dry for 24 hours. Turn the hearts over after 12 hours. Lightly sand the sides of the heart shapes with fine sandpaper.

Roll out two strips of paste. Brush the edge of the heart with egg whites. Attach one strip at a time. Trim off the excess with a pair of scissors. Attach the other strip and trim. Pipe lines of royal icing inside the box along the seams and base. Dip a small brush into egg whites and brush the whites over the royal icing to seal the box. Let dry for 24 hours. Repeat this for the box lid.

Use cameos and wooden molds to shape rolled fondant or gumpaste decorations.

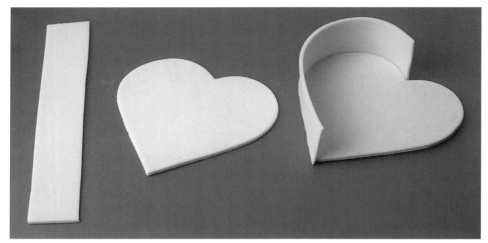

To create the heart box, begin with 4 strips and 2 heart shapes (one slightly larger than the other for the heart. A large heart is best made from pastillage. A small heart can be made from gumpaste, which will give you more time to work the paste before it hardens.

Use the pattern below.

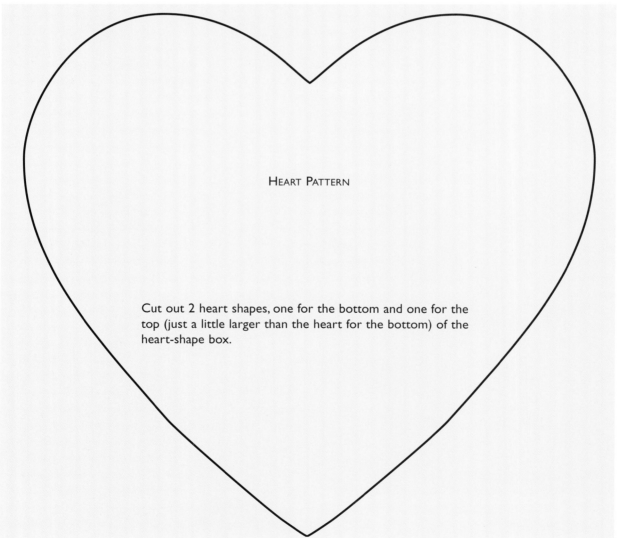

HEART PATTERN

Cut out 2 heart shapes, one for the bottom and one for the top (just a little larger than the heart for the bottom) of the heart-shape box.

Rolled Fondant Drapery

Well-executed rolled fondant drapery creates a lush, full, and beautiful effect like that of fabric draped over the cake. First, measure the cake and divide it into the number of sections needed for fondant drapes.

CLASSICAL DRAPERY To make the drapes, we suggest using commercial rolled fondant because it contains little traces of gum traga-canth which adds to the strength of the paste. You could also use gumpaste for drapery work. If you are using homemade rolled fondant, add ½ teaspoon of Tylose to 1 pound (454 g) of rolled fondant. Knead thoroughly and let the fondant rest in a zippered plastic bag 1 hour before use. The Tylose gives the rolled fondant more stretch and strength.

Roll out the fondant to ⅛ inch (3 mm) thick on a surface that has been rubbed with a little white vegetable shortening. Square off the fondant with a ruler and an X-acto knife. Cut the fondant about 1 inch (2.5 cm) wide. Determine the length of the strips to match the cake's

Swan's Neck & Head

The swan's neck is graceful and beautiful. You'll need a large piece of gumpaste to create it. Roll the gumpaste into a large cylinder. Immediately shape the beak and head of the swan. Let the shape dry on rubber foam to protect the other side of the swan. Let dry for 24 to 48 hours. Turn over and dry on the opposite side.

For the swan's neck, roll gumpaste into a cylinder, shape the beak and head, and let dry.

For classical drapery, use commercial rolled fondant or gumpaste. Roll it out and use a ruler and an X-acto knife to square it off and cut.

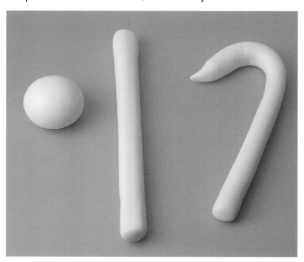

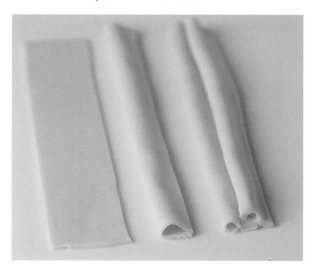

CLASSICAL DRAPERY

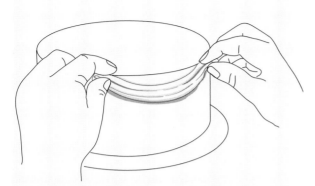

Prepare and wet the drape. Then wet the cake area where you plan to place the drape.

FREEHAND DRAPERY

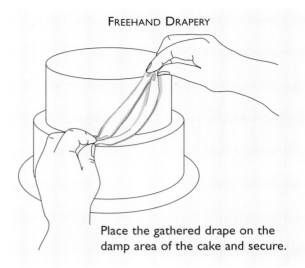

Place the gathered drape on the damp area of the cake and secure.

measurements. You'll need to cut two or three strips for a single drape.

When ready to assembly the drape, brush one end of the drape with water and fold over the other end, making sure that only the ends touch. Insert a long skewer into the back of the drape, maintaining the integrity of the cavity. Repeat this once or twice more. Brush water in the center of one of the folded strips. Place the second strip on top of the first strip, securing it to the damp area. If making a triple drape, repeat the second step.

With a damp paintbrush dipped in a little water, wet the area of the cake where the drape is to reside. Pick up both ends of the drape and attach the drape to the damp area on the cake. Pinch off the ends and secure the drape.

FREEHAND DRAPERY Roll out a large rectangular piece of rolled fondant. Cut and square off the paste. Tuck ends of both sides under the paste. Use a damp brush dipped into a little water to dampen the area on the cake where you want the drapery. Gather the paste in the center. Use your left and right hands, holding the drape between the thumb and middle finger of each hand. Use the index finger to keep the drape intact. Carefully place the drape on the damp area, securing and tapering the ends to the cake.

For freehand drapery, tuck the ends of both sides under the rolled out rectangle of fondant. When you're ready to transfer the drape to the damp area of the cake, gather the drape in the center, using your thumbs and middle fingers.

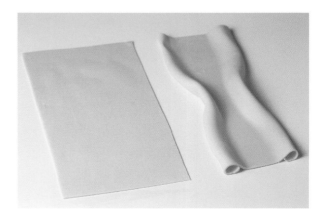

You can adorn freehand drapery with gumpaste flowers or buds as well as marzipan fruits or other shapes. Freehand drapery on this wedding cake (close-up above, full cake below) is so alluring that it could compete with the bride's dress for attention.

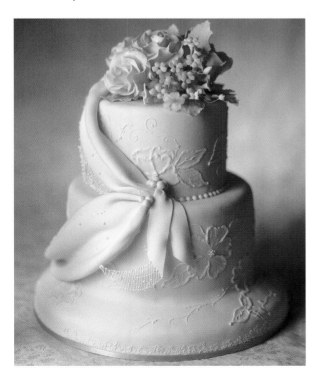

Modeling Chocolate Roses

Modeling chocolate roses are stunning. They are hand shaped without the use of cutters, although you can roll out the modeling chocolate paste, cut the petals with a cutter, and attach them to the base. Designed to elegantly finish the cake, these roses can transform a simple look into one that's breathtaking.

To make a medium-size rose, you need one white or dark-chocolate rose base and eight petal bases. For a full-size rose, you'll need one white or dark-chocolate rose base and fifteen petals.

First, make a base by rolling a piece of modeling chocolate about 1 inch (2.5 cm) in diameter. Put the chocolate between both hands and rotate your hands in opposite directions to create a round ball shape.

If you're right-handed, put the ball of chocolate in your left hand. With your right hand, apply light pressure with your index and middle fingers as you roll the ball back and forth, creating a tip at one end to form a cone shape. Place the finished shape in the cone-shaped Rose Base pattern to check for size (see p. 108). All eight balls should fit inside the pattern.

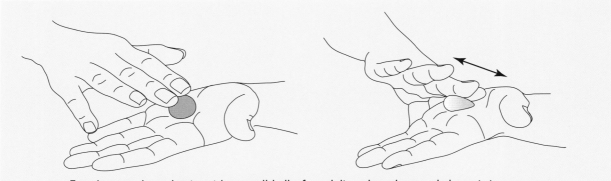

For the rose base, begin with a small ball of modeling chocolate, and shape it into a cone by rolling and lightly pressing with two fingers.

To make the first petal, put one of the balls on your work surface. Put a piece of heavy-duty plastic wrap, Mylar, or plastic kitchen zipper bag over the ball. With your thumb, beginning at the 9 o'clock position, apply light to heavy pressure as you move your thumb from the 9 to the 3 o'clock position. Shape the ball immediately to resemble a flat round shape, with the left side of the petal being heavy and the right side being very thin.

The petal's sides should be thin. Run your thumb around the sides of the petal for thinness. Remove the plastic by pulling from the heavy side to avoid tearing the petal. Put the petal inside the flattened Rose Petal Sizes (see drawings below);

the first eight petals should fit inside circle "8."

Place the first petal around the cone, raising the petal about one-third higher than the tip of the cone base. The petal's thin edge should be at the top. Wrap the petal around the cone, leaving a tiny hole at the top of the cone. The petal should only fit around the top to the middle of the cone-shaped rose base and not around the entire cone. Do not seal the edges yet.

Using the guides for flattened Rose Petal Sizes below, shape the next two petals as you did the first petal. After you have the correct flattened size, hold the petal by the bottom (the heavy side). Use your opposite hand to place it in back of the petal at the top center.

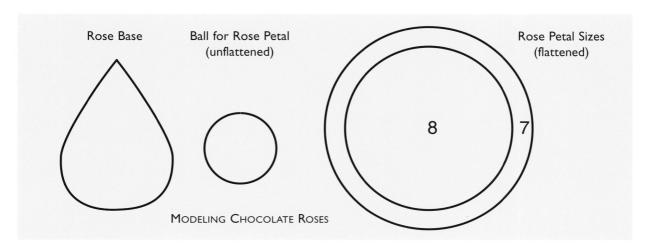

Rose Base

Ball for Rose Petal
(unflattened)

Rose Petal Sizes
(flattened)

8   7

MODELING CHOCOLATE ROSES

To assemble the modeling chocolate rose (top left to right), begin with a ball of modeling chocolate, and shape it into a cone. Make eight small petals and seven large petals. Attach the first petal to the center of the cone. Then begin overlapping petals by about one-third, tucking the latest petal inside the previous one.

For the modeling chocolate bow and streamers (center), cut out a flat bow shape from modeling chocolate rolled thin, creating gentle curved edges. (See Bow Pattern on p. 110.) Cut out a thin short strip for the "tie" and two long chocolate ribbon streamers.

Beginning at the center, pinch the top slightly and move your thumb and middle finger down the sides of the ball to the middle of the ball to form a rose petal. Move your fingers back to the top to go over the petal for a more realistic look. Repeat this procedure for the next petal.

Rosebud with three petals.

The first finished petal, remember, was placed over any seam in the cone and slightly higher than the cone. Place the second petal opposite the first and slightly higher than the cone. Overlap the sides of the petals, pressing lightly. As you overlap the sides, remember to keep the integrity of the folded sides for a more natural look. Now you can seal the bottom edges of the petals. You've created a rosebud.

Shape the next five petals. Attach the fourth petal over one of the rosebud seams. Do not seal in the edges, especially not the left side of the first petal you're attaching. Leave that side open. Attach the fifth petal, overlapping the fourth petal. The petal should overlap about one-third of the pre-

vious petal. Position the fifth petal to the right of the fourth petal, attaching it in a counterclockwise direction. Continue with the sixth and seventh petals, overlapping the previous petals. When attaching the eighth petal, overlap the seventh petal, and lift up the fourth petal (the first petal). Seal the eighth petal inside the fourth petal. Overlap the fourth petal on the eighth petal. You now have a medium-size bloom.

For a full-size bloom, shape seven more petals. The last seven rose petals should fit inside circle "7" of our pattern size. Place the petals, starting at any of the seams, slightly higher than the previous petals. Overlap the petals and continue as you did previously to create a full-blown rose.

A bouquet of white chocolate roses and rose leaves can make a sumptuous edible display on top of a cake. Each rose can take on its own character.

CHOCOLATE ROSE LEAVES

Roll out a piece of chocolate modeling paste as thinly as possible. If white chocolate, color the chocolate in a pale green or mint green. Cut some leaves by hand. To do this, position an X-acto knife at a 45° angle and cut oval shapes freehand. Or use any leaf shape cutter.

Score the leaves by dragging lines from the top to the bottom of the leaf with a skewer or rounded toothpick. Or press the back of a clean rose leaf on the chocolate, or press a silicone leaf press on the chocolate petal for texture.

Put the petal on a cell pad. Using a dogbone tool, soften the edge of the petal, giving some life to the shape.

BOW WITH STREAMERS

Roll out a piece of modeling chocolate paste as thinly as possible. Use the Bow Pattern below, place it over the chocolate, and carefully cut out the bow with an X-acto knife. Cut out two streamers freehand using a straight edge or ruler. Cut an upside-down "V" shape at the end of the streamers. Place a dot of water in the bow's center. Bring the ends together to the center of the bow. Cut a small strip of modeling chocolate and put it over the center of the bow or leave it plain. Turn the bow over and pinch and squeeze the center to complete the bow.

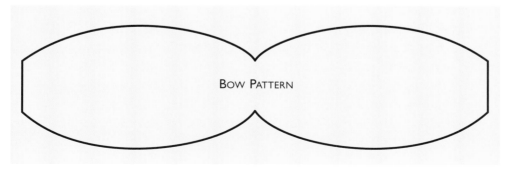

BOW PATTERN

CHAPTER 9

A Gallery of Cakes

We wanted to show a few of the many creative cake-design possibilities when using sugar products. The cakes in this photo gallery draw on a wide range of techniques demonstrated in Chapters 1 to 8. These designs are my own original interpretations of what I've learned through my years as a pastry artist and teacher.

Study techniques for buttercream, rolled icing, gumpaste flowers, bridgework, embroidery, mold presses, modeling chocolate, marzipan, piping, monogram, tiering, draping, gilding, and more to fashion your own style and design your own cakes. Borrow elements from one or more cake designs to create your own masterpiece.

Gilded Rose Cake

This cake is pretty enough and almost suitable for picture framing. The rolled-icing cake is covered in peach rolled fondant and the cake is small—no higher than 1 inch (2.5 cm). The centerpiece was created with a wooden press mold. Royal icing beads are piped around the mold and super pearl dust added for a realistic look. Hand-piped peach blossoms adorn the bottom and top of the mold as well as some fine freehand embroidery piping. The center of the mold is gilded in gold to give a lush look to the piece. Finally, a tapestry gold ribbon is tied around the cake to complete this lovely look.

Scrolls & Violets Cake

A fluid hand and raised scrolls define this cake covered in a bluish lavender color. The initial letter in the name is outlined and flooded in meringue powder flood icing for a raised look.

Before the icing dried, dots of white icing were piped on top and a toothpick dragged through the dots to create the pretty hearts in the lettering. The cake was lavished with overpiped scrolls and freehand embroidery. Hand-piped violets and a purple ribbon complete "Loreal."

Lovebirds' Engagement Cake

A whirlwind romance is the perfect setting for this intimate cake. The birds on top of the cake symbolize love and devotion, the round cake under the birds symbolizes eternity for the lucky couple, and the beautiful drapery ties the couple together. The cake is meticulously iced in white rolled fondant. The round cake on top can be baked in two half-mold pans and sandwiched together with icing or filling. The birds can be made by hand or molded in a small press. Freehand embroidery adorns the couple's monogram and scores of plunger flowers adorn the neck of the drum. Rolled fondant drapery and egg-white-royal-icing hearts pull this lovely ornamental cake together.

The lovebirds and plunger flowers sitting on the top of the cake were created from gumpaste.

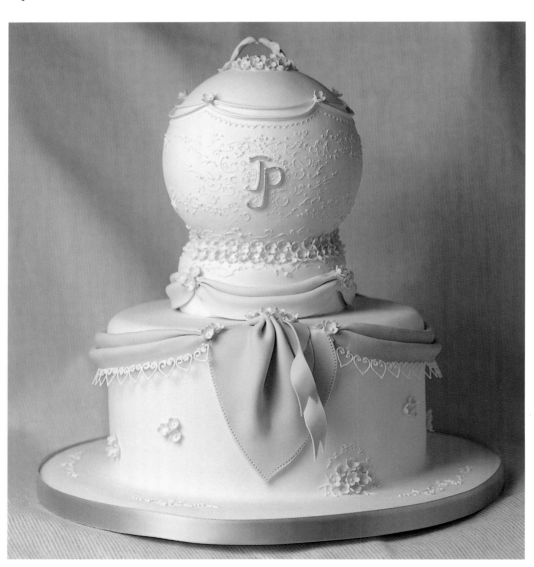

Wedding Drape Cake

"Beautiful and sexy" were the words my photographer used to describe this cake. It was originally designed for Kate Manchester's *The Perfect Wedding Cake* book. We loved this cake so much that we slightly updated the cake with more pulled blossoms on top and added a lovely "floating" lace band at the bottom of the ribbon drape.

The Wedding Drape Cake is adorned with beautiful brush embroidery and a bouquet of gumpaste flowers. Fondant drapes are lavishly added to accentuate the lush sensuality of the cake. Finally, the cake's bell shape is achieved by rolling a log of fondant that fits around the uniced cake. An offset metal spatula was used to blend the fondant to the cake board. Once iced, the cake has a bell-shaped appearance.

Fall Wedding Cake

A beautiful open rose with blossoms, brown buds, acorns, and foliage creates the backdrop for this lace appliqué wedding cake. The cake is made of oak-leaf appliqué made with rolled fondant. The fondant is rolled thin, cut with a cutter, and attached with water. Cornelli lace is piped inside some of the leaves and the leaves are embossed with a piece of fabric lace. Blown sugar balls and hand-shaped gold balls add richness to the cake along with a circle of hand-cut pastillage discs, decorated with pyramid dots.

Satin-Stitch Embroidery Cake

This beautifully iced cake can be a groom's cake, a small engagement-party cake, or an intimate wedding cake for a few lucky friends. It suggests the kind of fine embroidery found on elegant table linens and pillows. The mono-grams and floral motifs are piped in satin stitch. First outline the monograms and flood them. After they dry, pipe tiny lines back and forth to achieved this exquisite textured look.

The satin-stitch embroidery requires a steady hand and lots of rest between stitching, but the results are well worth it.

Three Stages of Mocha Iced Cakes

These Mocha Iced Cakes can be made in three stages or you can stop at the first or second stage, depending on your ability.

This first-stage cake couldn't be easier. The cake is covered in mocha-colored rolled fondant and crimped at the top edge. Beautiful lacy ribbons are tied around the cake, and a buttercream shell border finishes the cake.

In the second stage, the mocha cake has single stringwork around the top, and the inscription "Sara" also adorns it.

In the third and final stage, a double string is added around the cake's top edge and some "S" embroidery appears above the ribbons. The top of the cake also includes a dark modeling-chocolate rose and mocha-colored hand-shaped roses. The cake is complete with a bouquet of lacy ribbons behind the roses.

Ribbon Bouquet Anniversary Cake

Created in a grand style, this lushly decorated cake embodies elegance, femininity, and a lot of attention to detail. The hallmark technique used in this cake is the Australian stringwork. Classic to this style are the lines of stringwork piped to build up the bridge. Little dots of icing, called hail spotting, adorn some stringwork, and parts of the stringwork are raised with "side curtains." What also makes this cake unique are the overpiped lines at the bottom tier's top edge, which is classic to traditional English, notably the Lambeth style. Sugar cameos, plunger flowers, "S" scrolls, and embroidery piping give this cake its unique look. Finally, a cluster of sugar ribbons adorns the top of the cake for an elegant finish.

Victorian Rose Wedding Cake

Fit for a royal wedding or a head of state, this lavishly designed cake encompasses many of the techniques in this book. Most techniques used in the creation of this cake are done in the Lambeth or traditional 19th century English style of cake decorating. The lavish cushion lattice, overpiped "C" and "V" scrolls, drop stringwork, extension piping, flooded hearts, and scores of sugar flowers are just the beginning of this stately cake. The band of fondant around the middle of the cake is called a cylindrical roll. A large ball of rolled fondant is rolled into a log and fitted around the top edge of the cake. Fondant drapes and ribbons are added to comple-ment the roll. Sprays of gumpaste flowers are inserted into the roll (preventing the wire stems from going into the cake).

Both tiers are iced in antique rose meringue-powder royal icing. Filigree lace is piped, dried, and arranged with the gumpaste flowers. The top ornament on the cake was magical. We attached two-molded heart-shaped pieces of gumpaste to a flat gumpaste disk. Both molded shapes were attached with royal icing. A small, round platform was made from gumpaste. The heart-shaped ornament was attached to the round platform disc with royal icing. Gumpaste flowers were arranged around the bottom of the heart ornament and on top of the heart.

As the close-up of the detail work in the photo left shows, the Victorian style was replete with ornament. Above is a royal-iced cake board ornament. The photo at right displays this magnificent 19th century–style cake in its full glory.

The fun part was creating the shape of the swan and the magical couple. It took several days for head and neck to dry. The head and neck were made from gumpaste. The couple is made of gumpaste. The couple can be made of marzipan with gumpaste clothing. The heart-shaped cake represents the swan's body.

The bottom of the cake is Australian bridgework with small drop string on top. Above the strings are tiny "S" scrolls. The bridgework represents the swan in a sitting position looking "regal." Overpiped lines on the shoulders of the cake represent the swan's wings. The overpiped half-circles in the back of the swan represents the tail. Finally, the mice couple with tiny details and a small spray of sugar flowers complete the magic.

Swan Princess Cake

My son asked me to create this cake when he was a little boy. One of his favorite movies was *The Swan Princess.* Since it was a fairy tale, I wanted to create something that would look magical, airborne, and ethereal. This cake could be a small wedding cake or a beautiful engagement cake.

The swan's tail has overpiped half-circles and inverted hearts.

Wedding Dress Cake

Designed for *Bride's* magazine, this breathtaking cake resembles the finest details on a bride's dress. Lavish freehand embroidery piping and brush-embroidery piping begin the details in this dress. The bodice details are striking as well as the extension-work piping at the base of the petticoat. This is a one-of-a-kind cake for that special couple.

Rose Garden Wedding Cake

Sumptuously beautiful, this Rose Garden Wedding Cake is the perfect solution for a summer wedding. Richly adorned in hand-sculpted white-chocolate roses, this cake is covered in mint or moss-green and daffodil-yellow rolled icing. Beautiful brush painting accentuates the top shoulder of each tier. The rope border and tassels at the base of the bottom tier are made with a clay gun and commercial rolled icing. They perfectly complete this deliciously exciting confection.

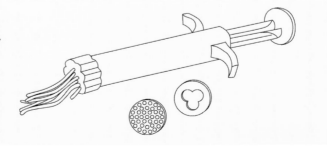

A clay gun like this one can be fitted with many disks, which allow you to pipe desired shapes. We used a disk similar to the one shown to create the rope border and tassels at the bottom of the Rose Garden Wedding Cake.

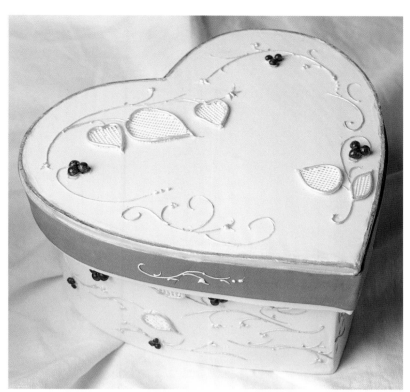

Cake-in-a-Box

Creating the sugar box was the most exciting part of this project. The pastillage box was decorated with lattice leaves, violet plums, and embroidery piping. The heart-shaped cake is iced in rolled icing and crimped at the top edge. The flower on top of the cake is brush embroidered with meringue-powder royal icing. Eat the cake and save the box as a remembered treasure.

Monogrammed Wedding Cake

Simply elegant are the words used to describe this monogrammed wedding cake. This cake was featured in the fall 1998 issue of *Bride's*. The cake also features fine stringwork on the top and bottom tiers. The middle tier contains sugar plaques with his, hers, and the couple's shared initials. Last, fondant drapes with bows and ribbons add to the cake's elegance along with the beautiful arrangement of sugar flowers on top.

Photo by Jeff Harris.

Artistic photo slants by Jeff Harris. Published with permission from Bride's magazine.

Photo by Wendell T. Webber. Published with permission from In Style Weddings, spring 2002.

Crystal Wedding Cake

Blown sugar balls and hand-shaped silvery white pearls adorn this classic white cake. This cake was featured in *In Style Weddings,* spring 2002 issue. Also featured on this snow-white cake is Australian stringwork with fine embroidery piping. Classic overpiped half-circles adorn the shoulders of this cake along with hand-shaped fondant pearl clusters. The center drum, decorated with lavish drapery and ribbon work, makes this cake the center of any celebration.

Marbleized Cake

This shades-of-color marbleized cake is lovely and savvy. Raspberry-flavor rolled icing on this almond-paste cake is most appealing. It can work wonders for any occasion.

Crown-of-Petals Cake

This luscious fruitcake, iced in marzipan and royal icing is the perfect finish to a Sunday brunch out in the country. A simpler version would be a yellow cake, iced in French Vanilla Butterceam and adorned with buttercream petals.

Cake Cachet

Stylized and buckled, this contemporary-looking cake is a fashion statement. This elegant cake features gold nuggets and gold inlay work. My photographer, Steven Mark Needham, named this confection; it was one of his favorite cakes.

Chocolate & Raspberry Cake

Chocolate and raspberries make simply the best taste combination ever. This chocolate-iced cake with hand-shaped raspberries made from marzipan makes this cake striking and inviting. Here's a hint: Brush your chocolate fudge layers with framboise liqueur and sandwich with chocolate buttercream. Finish the look with chocolate rolled icing. Serve this rich confection with whipped cream on the side.

Basket-of-Fruit Cake

A sumptuous basket-weave cake filled with hand-shaped marzipan fruits, berries, and leaves and rolled-fondant blossoms is elegant and appropriate anywhere and anytime. It's especially good if you make the lemon coconut cake and fill it with lemon curd. Basket-weave the cake with French vanilla buttercream or decorators' buttercream. (Find these and other delicious recipes in chapter 10.)

Holly & Lace Christmas Cake

This Holly & Lace Christmas Cake should inspire the Christmas spirit with its lavish gold decoration. This spectacular cake brings holiday cheer complete with holly, berries, a three-dimensional ornament attached with rope and tassels, and exquisite Cornelli-lace piping.

Sweet Smell of Orchid Cake

Present this confection to a couple cele-
brating their first anniversary. Exquisitely
piped, but simply adorned, this stunning
cake boasts a cymbidium orchid that's as
elegant and fresh as the young loving couple. The orchid was carefully constructed
from gumpaste.

Ingredients for Success

A MASTER CHEF'S SECRETS

Toba's Favorite Recipes

Icings

SWISS MERINGUE BUTTERCREAM

This classic buttercream icing is light, delicious, and buttery. It's not the best icing to choose in warm weather.

Ingredients

12 oz (336 g) egg whites (10 large egg whites or about 1½ cups)

3 cups (680 g) granulated sugar

3 lbs (1.36 kg) unsalted butter, room temperature

2 Tbsp lemon extract, almond extract, orange extract, *or* pure vanilla extract

or up to 3 fl oz (90 ml) light rum, framboise, pear William, or kirsch

1. Lightly whisk egg whites and sugar together over simmering water until egg-white mixture is hot to touch or a candy thermometer reads 140°F (60°C).

2. Pour hot whites into a room-temperature bowl and whip with a wire whip until double in volume on MEDIUM-HIGH speed. When the mixer stops, the meringue should not move around in the bowl. Meanwhile cut up butter into 2-inch pieces. (The butter should be slightly moist on the outside but cold inside.)

3. On your mixer, remove the whip and attach the paddle. Add half the butter (1½ lbs or 680 g) into the bowl immediately and pulsate the mixer several times until the meringue has covered the butter completely. To pulsate the mixer, turn it on and off in a jerky motion. This forces the butter on the top to the bottom of the bowl. Add the balance of the butter (1½ lbs or 680 g) and pulsate mixer several times. Slowly increase the mixer's speed, starting with the lowest speed and increase the speed every 10 seconds until you reach a MEDIUM-HIGH speed.

4. Continue beating until the mixture begins to look light and fluffy. Stop the mixer and scrape the bowl. Reduce speed to LOW. Add flavoring and continue to beat on LOW speed for 45 seconds. Then beat on MEDIUM-HIGH speed for an additional 45 to 60 seconds.

5. Leftover buttercream can be placed in plastic containers with lids and kept in the freezer for up to 3 months. Defrost completely (several hours) and rewhip before using.

Note: In hot weather, use 2 lbs 10 ounces (1.19 kg) of butter and 6 ounces (710 g) of hi-ratio shortening. Hi-ratio shortening is emulsified and contains water.

Storage: Store the icing in an airtight container and freeze for up to 3 months.

Yield: 2½ quarts (2.37 L)

AMARETTO MOCHA BUTTERCREAM

This is a delicious alternative to the Swiss Meringue Buttercream. It's a must for coffee addicts.

Ingredients

1 recipe Swiss Meringue Buttercream (without flavoring)
4 Tbsp instant espresso coffee
3 fl oz (90 ml) Amaretto

1. Put prepared Swiss Meringue Buttercream in the bowl of a mixer. Turn the mixer on STIR speed with a paddle attachment.
2. In a separate small bowl, thoroughly whisk coffee and Amaretto until the coffee is dissolved. Slowly pour the coffee mixture into the prepared Swiss Meringue Buttercream. Beat on MEDIUM-HIGH speed for 2 to 3 minutes.
3. Stir with rubber spatula until thoroughly combined.
Variations: For alcohol sensitivity, substitute 1½ fl oz (45 ml) almond extract and 1½ fl oz (45 ml) water for the Amaretto.
Storage: Store the icing in an airtight container and freeze for up to 3 months.
Yield: 2¾ quarts (2.6 L)

AMARETTO PRALINE MOCHA BUTTERCREAM

This is another variation on Swiss Meringue Buttercream. It's a great treat for icing lovers.

Ingredients

1 recipe Amaretto Mocha Buttercream
4 to 6 oz (112 to 168 g) Praline Paste

On slow speed, mix Praline Paste into the prepared Amaretto Mocha Buttercream. Increase the speed and beat for 2 to 3 minutes.
Storage: Store the icing in an airtight container and freeze for up to 3 months.
Yield: 3 quarts (2.8 L)

WHITE CHOCOLATE BUTTERCREAM

White ganache makes this the best variation of Swiss Meringue Buttercream. It's sinfully delicious, ices well, and piped borders made with it look heavenly.

Ingredients

1 recipe Swiss Meringue Buttercream (without flavoring)
1½ to 2 cups (345 to 454 g) refrigerated white Ganache

1. Make the Swiss Meringue Buttercream and the Ganache, using white chocolate. (See recipes on pp. 134 and 138.)
2. Turn the mixer on SLOW speed. Add white ganache ½ cup at a time to the Swiss Meringue Buttercream. Add more white Ganache until you achieve the desired flavor.
Storage: Store the icing in an airtight container and freeze. The icing will keep for up to 2 months.
Yield: 3 quarts (2.8 L)

DECORATOR'S BUTTERCREAM ICING

This decorator's staple remains an old reliable when all else fails. It even performs well in warm weather.

Ingredients

2 cups (1 lb or 454 g) unsalted butter, room temperature
1 cup (230 g) vegetable shortening or hi-ratio shortening
1 Tbsp fresh lemon juice
    or 1½ tsp lemon extract, pure vanilla extract, or almond extract
3 lbs (1.36 kg) 10X confectioners' sugar
½ cup + 1 Tbsp (4½ fl oz or 135 ml) water, milk, or clear liqueur
3 Tbsp meringue powder
1 tsp salt

1. Cream shortening and butter with an electric, handheld, or paddle-whip mixer. Add flavoring and salt. Gradually add sugar, one cup at a time. Add meringue powder. (The mixture will appear dry.)

2. Add liquid of choice and beat until light and fluffy (approximately 5 to 8 minutes). Keep the bowl covered with a damp cloth or plastic wrap.

Storage: Store the icing in an airtight container and freeze for up to 3 months.

Yield: 2½ quarts (2.37 L)

MASTER CHEF'S HINT

Add extra liquid to soften the buttercream or extra 10X confectioners' sugar to stiffen it.

BUTTERCREAM ICING FOR PIPED ROSES

Your roses will taste as good as the icing on the cake when piped with this buttercream.

Ingredients

2½ cups (1¼ lb or 569 g) unsalted butter, room temperature

½ cup (115 g) vegetable or hi-ratio shortening

1 Tbsp fresh lemon juice *or* 1½ tsp lemon extract *or* 1½ tsp almond extract

1 Tbsp water *or* milk

3 lbs (1.36 kg) 10X confectioners' sugar

3 Tbsp meringue powder

1 tsp salt

Follow procedures for making Decorator's Buttercream Icing. If the icing is too stiff, add drops of water or milk to a small bowl of the icing.

Storage: Store the icing in an airtight container and freeze for up to 3 months.

Yield: 2¼ quarts (2.14 L)

DECORATOR'S BUTTERCREAM PRACTICE ICING

Use this icing for practice only. It lasts for months without refrigeration.

Ingredients

1 cup (230 g) vegetable shortening

3 to 4 Tbsp water

1 lb (454 g) 10X confectioners' sugar

1 Tbsp meringue powder

Follow procedures for making Decorator's Buttercream Icing. Beat for 8 to 12 minutes. The recipe may be duplicated as many times as needed. Icing DOES NOT need to be refrigerated!

Storage: Store the icing in an airtight container with a plastic lid; it will keep for 2 months. You do not need to refrigerate it.

Yield: 3 to 3½ cups (720 to 840 ml or about 685 to 800 g)

CHOCOLATE BUTTERCREAM

This is the best chocolate buttercream icing ever. The icing is rich, like mousse, and outrageously delicious.

Ingredients

2 cups (1 lb or 454 g) unsalted butter, room temperature

½ cup (115 g) vegetable shortening

3 lbs (1.36 kg) 10X confectioners' sugar

1 cup (110 g) Dutch processed cocoa powder

3 Tbsp meringue powder

1 tsp salt

5 fl oz (150 ml) chocolate liqueur (i.e., Godiva or another)

2 Tbsp milk

1 Tbsp pure vanilla extract

2 cups (1 lb or 454 g) refrigerated Ganache

1. First, prepare the Ganache. (See recipe on p.138.) Refrigerate until firm.

2. Cream the butter and shortening for 2 minutes. Stop to scrape the bowl. Cream the mixture for an additional 60 seconds.

3. Sieve cocoa powder and confectioners' sugar together. Add the sugar mixture 1 cup at a time to the creamed butter and shortening. Mix until well blended. Add meringue powder and salt and beat for one minute. Mixture will appear dry.

4. Add milk, vanilla extract, and chocolate liqueur to the buttercream. Beat until well combined.

5. Add Ganache, 1 cup at a time and beat until light and fluffy.

Storage: Store the icing in an airtight container and freeze. The icing will keep for up to 2 months.

Yield: 2½ to 3 quarts (2.37 to 2.85 L)

FRENCH VANILLA BUTTERCREAM

This is simply the most delicious icing ever. It tastes like vanilla ice cream. Use this icing when looking for something similar to whipped cream.

Ingredients

1½ cups (345 g) granulated sugar

¾ cup (6 fl oz or 180 ml) milk

1½ Tbsp all-purpose flour

¼ tsp salt

1 Tbsp pure vanilla extract

⅜ cup (3 fl oz or 90 ml) whipping cream

1¼ lbs (567 g) unsalted butter, room temperature

1. Make custard by heating milk and sugar until sugar crystals dissolve. Add flour and salt and whisk over an ice bath until the custard has cooled, or cover with plastic wrap and refrigerate for ½ hour to cool the mixture. Whisk in vanilla extract.

2. Pour the custard mixture into a mixer bowl with a paddle attachment. Add cut-up butter and add whipping cream. Mix on LOW speed to incorporate ingredients. Gradually increase speed to MEDIUM-HIGH until the mixture begins to thicken. It takes at least 7 to 9 minutes for the butter to be completely incorporated.

3. Put the icing in a plastic container with a lid and refrigerate. It will keep for 1 week in the refrigerator or freeze for 2 months.

Note: Don't panic if the buttercream looks like cottage cheese. The more you beat this buttercream, the creamier it gets.

Storage: Store the icing in an airtight container and freeze. The icing will keep for up to 2 months.

Yield: 5 to 6 cups (1.2 to 1.4 L) or 2½ to 3 lbs (1.2 to 1.3 kg)

CREAM CHEESE BUTTERCREAM

The tangy flavor of this buttercream is great with any cake, but especially carrot or peanut butter cake.

Ingredients

1 cup (8 oz or 230 g) unsalted butter, room temperature

2 oz (56 g) solid vegetable shortening

10 oz (280 g) cream cheese, *or* 5 oz (140 g) mascarpone cheese and 5 oz (140 g) regular cream cheese

1½ lbs (680 g) 10X confectioners' sugar

2 Tbsp (1 fl oz or 30 ml) heavy cream

1 tsp vanilla extract

2 tsp fresh lemon juice

1 Tbsp meringue powder

1. Cream butter, shortening, and cream cheese together for 3 minutes. Stop and scrape the bowl. Cream for an additional 60 seconds.

2. Add sugar 1 cup at a time to the cream mixture. Add meringue powder, heavy cream, vanilla extract, and lemon juice. Beat for 3 minutes, making sure that the ingredients are thoroughly incorporated. Stop, scrape the bowl, and beat for 1 minute more.

3. Store in plastic containers with lids and place them in the refrigerator. This icing will keep for 2 weeks, or freeze for up to 2 months.

Storage: Store the icing in an airtight container and freeze. The icing will keep for up to 2 months.

Yield: 1½ quarts (1.4 L)

GANACHE

This chocolate cream icing is a pastry chef's staple. Use it to glaze a cake or, when it cools, whip it to a piping consistency.

Ingredients

1½ cups (12 fl oz or 360 ml) heavy cream
1 lb (454 g) semisweet or bittersweet dark
    chocolate

1. In a heavy saucepan, boil heavy cream. Turn off the heat. Add chopped chocolate pieces and let it rest until melted. Use a rubber spatula to stir the mixture until all the pieces are melted.

2. Pour it into a room-temperature bowl and cover with plastic wrap. Refrigerate the ganache until firm.

Note: For White Chocolate Ganache, substitute white chocolate for semisweet or bittersweet dark chocolate.

Storage: Store the icing in an airtight container and refrigerate. The icing will keep for up to 2 weeks in the refrigerator.

Yield: 3½ cups (800 g)

EGG-WHITE ROYAL ICING

Use Egg-White Royal Icing for piping on rolled iced cakes and as an ornamental icing.

Ingredients

3 oz (84 g) fresh egg whites or pasteurized egg
    whites, room temperature
1 lb (454 g) 10X confectioners' sugar, sifted
½ tsp lemon juice

Lightly whip the egg whites on MEDIUM speed, using a paddle until the whites form soft peaks, about 3 minutes. Lower the speed and gradually add the sugar 1 cup (4 oz or 112 g) at a time. Add lemon juice and beat on MEDIUM-HIGH speed for 5 to 8 minutes, or until the icing forms medium to stiff peaks. Cover the icing with plastic wrap until it's ready to use.

Note: This icing should be used within 1 day. For individuals sensitive to egg whites or to avoid possible salmonella food poisoning, use only pasteurized egg whites, or use the recipe for Meringue Powder Royal Icing instead.

Storage: Use within 1 day or store the icing in an airtight container with plastic wrap directly over the icing and refrigerate for up to 3 days. Beat with a metal spatula before using.

Yield: 5 cups (1.2 L) or 2.5 lbs (1.15 kg)

MERINGUE POWDER ROYAL ICING

This is an alternative to egg-white or pasteurized Egg-White Royal Icing.

Ingredients

¼ cup (1.6 oz or 45 g) meringue powder
½ cup (120 ml) cold water
1 lb (454 g) 10X confectioners' sugar, sifted
½ tsp lemon juice

Add meringue powder to cold water in a mixing bowl. Beat to a soft peak stage—about 3 minutes. Add the confectioners' sugar 1 cup (4 oz or 112 g) at a time. Beat between each cup. Add the lemon juice. Beat for an additional 3 to 5 minutes on MEDIUM-HIGH speed or until the icing forms medium to stiff peaks. Cover with plastic wrap until ready to use.

Storage: Store the icing in an airtight container. Use a brand-new plastic container with a lid or a grease-free glass container. Meringue Powder Royal Icing can stay at room temperature for 2 weeks or it will keep in the refrigerator for up to 2 months. Beat before using.

Yield: 5 to 6 cups (1.2 to 1.4 L) or 2½ to 3 lbs (1.15 to 1.38 kg)

MERINGUE POWDER FLOOD ICING

Use this icing for flooding projects.

Ingredients

1 cup (240 ml) Meringue Powder Royal Icing
⅛ to ¼ cup (1 to 2 fl oz or 30 to 60 ml) water
   or pasteurized egg whites

Carefully stir the water into the Meringue Powder Royal Icing a little at a time. After adding half the water, check to see if you have the right consistency. Continue to add water until you have achieved a flow consistency. Add more liquid if necessary.

HOW TO CHECK FOR FLOW CONSISTENCY
You have achieved a flow consistency if, after you draw a knife through the icing, the icing completely comes back together after you count to 10 seconds. If the icing comes together before 7 seconds, add a little more Meringue Powder Royal Icing to thicken it. Check for consistency again. If the icing does not come together within 10 seconds, add a little more water.

Storage: Store the icing in a glass container and cover it with plastic wrap directly on the icing. Put a tight-fitting lid on the container. Use it within 3 to 5 days. This can be stored at room temperature. If refrigerated, use Meringue Powder Flood Icing within 1 week. Stir gently before using.

Yield: 1¼ cups (300 ml) or 10 oz (285 g)

ROLLED FONDANT

This icing gives a satin-smooth finish to the cake. When made from scratch, you control the ingredients and taste. Commercial brands are also available. This icing is not as palatable as other icings.

Ingredients

1 Tbsp (1 envelope) unflavored gelatin
¼ cup (60 ml) cold water
1 tsp lemon extract, almond extract, or orange
   extract
½ cup (6 oz or 168 g) light corn syrup
1 Tbsp glycerin (optional)
up to 2 lbs (908 g) 10X confectioners' sugar
½ tsp white vegetable shortening

1. Sprinkle the gelatin over cold water in a small bowl. Let it stand for two minutes to soften. Place it over a pan of simmering water until the gelatin dissolves, or use the microwave for 30 seconds on HIGH. Do not overheat. Add the flavoring.

2. Add corn syrup and glycerin and stir until mixture is smooth and clear. Gently reheat if necessary, or microwave for an additional 15 to 20 seconds on HIGH. Stir again.

3. Sift 1½ pounds (680 g) of the confectioners' sugar into a large bowl. Make a well in the sugar and pour in the liquid mixture. Stir with a wooden spoon. The mixture will become sticky.

4. Sift some of the remaining ½ pound (225 g) of sugar onto a smooth work surface and add as much of the remaining sugar as the mixture will take. Knead the fondant, adding more confectioners' sugar, if necessary, to form a smooth, pliable mass. The fondant should be firm but soft. Rub the vegetable shortening into your palms and knead it into the fondant. This relieves the stickiness of the fondant.

5. Wrap the fondant tightly in plastic wrap and place it in the refrigerator until ready to use. Rolled fondant works best if allowed to rest for 24 hours.

Note: If covered well, this rolled fondant dough can be refrigerated for 1 month or be frozen for up to 3 months. I do, however, recommend Pettinice RTR Icing (commercial rolled fondant). It doesn't taste quite as good as a homemade; however, it has more stretch. Since it's extremely flexible, you can do more with it. This product can last for up to 6 months without refrigeration.

Storage: Double wrap the rolled fondant in plastic wrap and then store it in a zippered plastic bag. It will keep in the refrigerator for 30 days or in the freezer for up to 3 months.

Yield: 2 lbs (908 g)

CHOCOLATE ROLLED FONDANT

Chocolate rolled fondant is a better-tasting icing than traditional "white" rolled fondant.

Ingredients

8 oz (224 g) Pettinice RTR Icing *or* homemade Rolled Fondant
2 to 5 Tbsp (0.2 to 0.6 oz or 6 to 16 g) cocoa powder
¼ to ½ tsp white vegetable shortening

1. Knead the fondant. Make a well in the center. Add 2 tablespoons of the cocoa powder. Knead thoroughly. Add more, a little at a time, until the paste starts to thicken and becomes slightly dry. Stop adding the cocoa powder. Knead thoroughly. Rub the white vegetable shortening into your palms and knead into the fondant. Knead until fondant is pliable.

2. Wrap it in plastic wrap and refrigerate until ready to use. This will last for weeks in the refrigerator. The recipe can be doubled or tripled.

Storage: Double wrap the chocolate rolled fondant in plastic wrap and then store it in a zippered plastic bag. It will keep in the refrigerator for 30 days or in the freezer for up to 3 months.

Yield: 8 oz (½ lb or 224 g) icing

MARZIPAN

This is a delicious alternative to rolled fondant icing. Its only drawback is its lack of stretch. See Note for making this icing creamier and with more stretch.

Ingredients

1 lb (454 g) almond paste
1 lb (454 g) 10X confectioners' sugar
3 fl oz (90 ml) or 4.5 oz (126 g) light corn syrup
1 tsp pure vanilla extract
1 tsp light rum

1. Cut up the almond paste and place it in a mixing bowl with paddle attachment. Beat on low speed for 2 minutes. Add half of the sugar and beat just until combined. Add corn syrup, vanilla and rum. Beat until combined.

2. Sprinkle the balance of the sugar onto a counter top. Add the paste and knead in all the sugar until the paste is smooth and pliable.

Note: For marzipan with extra stretch and a creamier taste—mix 2 parts Marzipan with 1 part commercial rolled fondant. Use a little powdered sugar to prevent sticking. Wrap in plastic wrap and refrigerate until ready to use.

Storage: Double wrap the marzipan in plastic

wrap and then store it in a zippered plastic bag. It will keep in the refrigerator for 30 days or in the freezer for up to 3 months.
Yield: 2¼ lbs (1 kg)

QUICK GUMPASTE

This quick and simple recipe always works. Use this for making lifelike flowers and for ribbons, bows, and drapery work.

Ingredients
1 lb (454 g) commercial rolled fondant (or homemade)
1½ tsp Tylose if commercial brand
  or 2 tsp Tylose if homemade
½ tsp white vegetable shortening

Make a well in the center of the rolled fondant. Add the Tylose. Rub the vegetable shortening into your palms and begin kneading the paste for a full 3 to 5 minutes. Double wrap in plastic wrap and let rest in the refrigerator until ready to use.
Note: This paste can be used immediately. However, it works best when aged for 24 hours in the refrigerator.
Storage: Double wrap the gumpaste in plastic wrap and store it in a zippered plastic bag. It will keep in the refrigerator for 4 to 6 months.
Yield: 1 lb (454 g)

PASTILLAGE

This ornamental icing can be used for building three-dimensional structures.

Ingredients
7 oz (about 200 g) Egg-White Royal Icing
2 tsp Tylose
2 to 3 Tbsp cornstarch

1. First, make a half-recipe of Egg-White Royal Icing (approximately 7 oz or 200 g).
2. In a medium-size bowl, measure out 7 ounces of icing. Add the Tylose to the royal icing. Stir vigorously until the texture begins to change and thickens.
3. Turn out onto the cornstarch and knead until firm but pliable. Add more cornstarch if needed, 1 tablespoon at a time.
4. Double wrap the pastillage in plastic wrap; then store the pastillage in a plastic zippered bag. You can use this paste immediately.
Note: This paste tends to dry very quickly. To make the paste more pliable, add 2 to 3 ounces of commercial rolled fondant. This will allow you to work a little longer before the pastillage dries.
Storage: Double wrap the pastillage in plastic wrap and store it in a zippered plastic bag. Refrigerate for up to 30 days.
Yield: 7½ oz (210 g)

MODELING CHOCOLATES
These delicious chocolates work best for hand-modeling projects. This common recipe has many variations. Modeling chocolate is also called chocolate plastic or chocolate plastique.

DARK MODELING CHOCOLATE
Ingredients
1 lb (454 g) semisweet or bittersweet dark chocolate
⅔ cup (8 oz or 224 g) light corn syrup

WHITE AND MILK MODELING CHOCOLATE
Ingredients
1 lb (454 g) white or mild chocolate
½ cup (6 oz or 168 g) light corn syrup

1. Cut up the chocolate finely and place it in a stainless-steel bowl over a pot of boiling water. Turn off the heat under the boiling water. Let the chocolate melt, stirring occasionally until the chocolate is two-thirds melted.

2. Remove it from the pot and stir it with a rubber spatula until it is completely melted. Pour in the corn syrup all at once and stir until the chocolate thickens and begins to leave the sides of the bowl.

3. Pour the chocolate into plastic wrap. Place another sheet of plastic wrap over the chocolate and flatten it out. Refrigerate for 24 hours to age.

4. Once aged, take it out of the refrigerator and let it sit for 30 minutes. Cut the modeling chocolate into pieces and knead it with your palms. If the chocolate is too hard to knead, wrap it in a piece of plastic wrap and microwave for 5 to 10 seconds on HIGH. Reknead until the chocolate is pliable.

5. Wrap pliable pieces in zippered plastic bags. When all the chocolate is pliable, reknead it until the chocolate turns a beautiful shiny color. Roll and cut the modeling chocolate to make ribbons and roses.

Note: Because of the fat content in the white and milk chocolates, don't over-stir the chocolate when you add in the corn syrup. Stir white or milk chocolate briefly, then pour the chocolate onto newsprint* to flatten it out. Let it rest for 2 to 4 hours to absorb some of the fat. Scrape the chocolate from the paper and lightly knead. Wrap it tightly in plastic wrap and refrigerate for 24 hours.

* Newsprint is an inexpensive paper that happens to absorb fat. You'll find it at art-supply stores.

Storage: Double wrap the modeling chocolate in plastic wrap and store it in a zippered plastic bag. It will keep in the refrigerator for 4 to 6 months.

Yield: 22 oz (616 g) dark modeling chocolate 20 oz (560 g) white and milk modeling chocolate

Cakes

CHOCOLATE FUDGE CAKE

This is the best chocolate cake ever. It's delicious to the last crumb.

Ingredients
2½ cups (287 g) all-purpose flour
1¼ cups (285 g) granulated sugar
¾ cup (170 g) dark brown sugar, packed
1 cup (110 g) Dutch processed cocoa powder
2¼ tsp baking soda
1½ tsp salt
2¼ cups (18 fl oz or 540 ml) buttermilk
1 cup (230 g) unsalted butter, room
  temperature
2 large eggs
1½ tsp pure vanilla extract
6 oz (168 g) melted semisweet fine quality
  chocolate

1. Heat oven to 350°F (175°C). Butter and parchment line two 8x2-inch (20x5-cm) baking pans.

2. Measure all ingredients (except the chocolate) into a large mixer bowl.

3. Blend for 30 seconds on LOW speed, scraping bowl constantly.

4. Blend in the melted chocolate and beat 3 minutes on HIGH speed, scraping the bowl.

5. Spoon into the pans and level them well with an offset spatula.

6. Bake layers for 45 to 50 minutes or until a toothpick inserted comes out clean.

Storage: Double wrap the cake in plastic wrap. It will keep in the refrigerator for up to 2 weeks or in the freezer for up to 2 months.

Yield: two 8-inch (20-cm) cakes

MOIST YELLOW CAKE

This is my favorite recipe in the book. I use this cake more than 85% of the time. It's always delicious. The Soft as Silk brand of cake flour gives best results.

Ingredients

3 cups (330 g) cake flour
1 Tbsp baking powder
½ tsp salt
1 cup (8 oz or 230 g) unsalted butter, room temperature
2 cups (454 g) granulated sugar
5 large eggs
2 tsp vanilla extract
1¼ cups (10 fl oz or 300 ml) buttermilk

1. Preheat oven to 350°F (175°C). Butter and line with parchment paper two 8x2-inch (20x5-cm) pans. Set aside.
2. In a medium bowl, sift together the flour, baking powder, and salt.
3. Cut up the butter into 1-inch pieces and place them in the large bowl of an electric mixer, fitted with a paddle attachment or beaters. Beat for 3 minutes on MEDIUM-HIGH speed until the butter is light and creamy in color. Stop and scrape the bowl. Cream the butter for an additional 60 seconds.
4. Add the sugar, ¼ cup at a time, beating 1 minute after each addition. Scrape the sides of the bowl occasionally. Add the eggs one at a time.
5. Reduce the mixer speed. Stir vanilla into the buttermilk. Add the dry ingredients alternately with the buttermilk. Mix just until incorporated. Scrape the sides of the bowl and mix for 15 seconds longer.
6. Spoon the batter into the prepared pan and smooth the top with a knife. Lift up the pan with the batter, and let it drop onto the counter top to burst any air bubbles, allowing the batter to settle.

7. Center the pans onto the lower third of the oven and let bake 45 to 50 minutes or until the cake is lightly brown on top and comes away from the sides of the pan and a toothpick inserted in the center comes out clean.
Note: Let the cake cool in the pan.
Storage: Double wrap the cake in plastic wrap. It will keep in the refrigerator for up to 2 weeks or in the freezer for up to 2 months.
Yield: two 8-inch (20-cm) cakes

APPLESAUCE FRUITCAKE
with Lacing Sauce

This delicious fruitcake is a wonderful diversion from the usual citron and candied fruit fruitcakes.

Ingredients

2 cups (460 g) dates, pitted
1 cup (230 g) prunes, pitted
1 cup (230 g) raisins
1½ cups (345 g) pecans
1½ cups (345 g) walnuts
3 cups (330 g) all-purpose flour
2 tsp baking soda
1 tsp baking powder
½ tsp cloves
½ tsp nutmeg
1 tsp cinnamon
½ tsp salt
½ cup (115 g) butter, room temperature
½ cup (115 g) light brown sugar, packed
½ cup (115 g) granulated sugar
1 Tbsp vanilla
2 eggs
½ cup (4 fl oz or 120 ml) white grape juice
2 cups (1 lb or 454 g) applesauce
4 oz (114 g) jar maraschino cherries, halved
½ cup (4 fl oz or 120 ml) white rum or brandy

1. Cut up the fruit and coarsely chop the nuts. Mix fruit and nuts together.

2. Sift flour, baking soda, baking powder, spices, and salt together. Set aside.

3. Cream the butter and sugar for 2 minutes. Add vanilla. Add eggs one at a time. Alternately add the dry ingredients and grape juice until blended. Mix in fruit, nuts, and applesauce. Stir in rum or brandy.

4. Line the bottom and sides of a 10x4-inch (25x10-cm) or a 12x3-inch (30x7.5-cm) pan with heavy brown paper. (The brown paper should be lightly sprayed with oil or vegetable spray before lining. Extend the paper on the sides of the pan by 2 to 3 inches (5 to 7.5 cm) higher than the height of the pan.)

5. Pour the batter into the pan and work evenly into corners. Lift up the pan with batter and let it drop onto counter to level the surface and break up any air bubbles.

6. Bake at 275°F (135°C) about 3 to 3½ hours or until toothpick inserted into the center comes out clean.

7. Leave in the brown paper wrappings until ready to ice.

Storage: Double wrap the applesauce fruit-cake in plastic wrap. Lace the fruitcake in the Lacing Sauce once a week for 6 to 8 weeks. Rewrap the fruitcake after lacing. DO NOT store it in the refrigerator. It will last for months.

Yield: 10x4-inch (25x10-cm) or 12x3-inch (30x7.5-cm) cake

LACING SAUCE

Ingredients

¼ cup (2 fl oz or 60 ml) maraschino cherry juice
½ cup (4 fl oz or 120 ml) white grape juice
½ cup (4 fl oz or 120 ml) pineapple juice
1 tsp pure vanilla extract
1 cup (8 fl oz or 240 ml) rum or brandy

1. Mix all ingredients together. Generously brush the liquid over the fruitcake, including the brown paper wrappings, using 2 fl oz of the liquid at each soaking.

2. Soak the cake once a week for 3 to 6 weeks.

3. After each soaking, wrap the entire cake, including the brown paper, in plastic wrap and put it back into the baking pan to keep the shape of the cake.

4. Store the cake in a dry place. DO NOT REFRIGERATE. Wait at least 3 weeks before icing and eating the iced fruitcake. Six weeks is best.

Storage: Store the lacing sauce in an airtight container in the pantry or in the refrigerator. It will keep for several weeks.

Yield: 2¼ cups (540 ml) lacing sauce

ALMOND-PASTE CAKE

This is my second favorite cake in the book.

Ingredients

6 oz (168 g) unsalted butter, room temperature
4 oz (114 g) almond paste
2 cups (454 g) granulated sugar
4 large eggs
1 tsp almond extract
1 cup (8 fl oz or 240 ml) whole milk
2½ cups (287 g) cake flour
1 Tbsp baking powder
½ tsp salt

1. Preheat oven to 350°F (175°C). Butter two 7-inch cake pans or one 10-inch cake pan and line with parchment paper. Set aside.

2. Cream the butter, almond paste, and sugar for 4 minutes. Stop, scrape the bowl, and cream for 60 seconds more.

3. Add eggs, one at a time, to the creamed mixture. Beat in the almond extract.

4. Sieve together the flour, salt, and baking powder. Alternately add the flour mixture and milk to the creamed mixture. Ladle the mixture into the baking pan. This is a thick batter.

Carefully smooth the batter with a metal offset spatula. Hit the pan against the counter to burst any air bubbles.

5. Bake in the center of oven for 45 minutes or until the cake slightly shrinks and a toothpick inserted in the center comes out clean.

Storage: The almond-paste cake freezes well and can last for 3 weeks in the refrigerator.

Yield: two 7-inch (18-cm) cakes or one 10-inch (25-cm) cake

DOMINICAN CAKE
WITH MERINGUE ICING

This fabulous Dominican cake and icing recipe comes from my good friend Isabel Acosta. I took copious notes as I watched her make this delectable confection.

Ingredients

1 lb (454 g) unsalted butter, room temperature

2 cups (1 lb or 454 g) granulated sugar, less 3 Tbsp to use later

4 cups (1 lb or 454 g) cake flour

12 extra-large egg yolks and 4 extra-large egg whites *(Put aside the 8 extra large whites for the icing.)*

1 Tbsp baking powder

1 Tbsp light rum

1 Tbsp Dominican vanilla, Bourbon, *or* Madagascar vanilla

¼ tsp salt

1 cup (8 fl oz or 240 ml) whole milk or pineapple juice

2 Tbsp cornstarch

1 Tbsp lemon zest

1. Preheat oven to 350ºF (175ºC). Prepare two 10-inch (25-cm) pans, brushed with butter and lined with parchment paper.

2. Cream the butter on LOW speed (2 minutes). Add the sugar and cream for 3 minutes. Stop, scrape the bowl, and cream for an additional 2 minutes. The mixture should be light and creamy.

3. In a separate bowl, mix all the dry ingredients (cake flour, baking powder, salt, and cornstarch). Sift the mixture twice. Meanwhile in another separate bowl, mix milk (or juice), rum, and vanilla together and hold it aside.

4. On LOW speed, add yolks one at a time to the creamed butter and sugar mixture. Mix until the yolks disappear. Alternately, add the flour and liquid mixture in three turns, starting with the flour. Add lemon zest and mix an additional 30 seconds.

5. In a separate bowl, beat the 4 extra-large egg whites until stiff (but not too dry), about 3 minutes on HIGH speed. At the end of 2 minutes of beating, add the 3 tablespoons of sugar. Beat for an additional 60 seconds.

6. Carefully fold whites into the cake batter. Pour the batter into prepared pans (two-thirds full). Bake in the center of the oven for 45 to 50 minutes, or until the cake slightly shrinks from the pan and a toothpick inserted in the center comes out clean.

Storage: Dominican Cake will last up to 2 weeks in the refrigerator.

Yield: two 10-inch (25-cm) cakes

MERINGUE ICING
FOR DOMINICAN CAKE

This shiny and glossy icing ices and pipes well.

Ingredients

¾ cup (6 fl oz or 180 ml) water

3 cups (690 g) granulated sugar, plus 2 Tbsp to use later

8 extra-large egg whites *(left from the Dominican cake)*

1 tsp Dominican vanilla, Bourbon, *or* Madagascar vanilla

1. Cook the water and sugar. When the syrup begins to boil, start beating the egg whites. Stop, add the 2 tablespoons of sugar to the egg whites, and continue to beat. Beat until medium to stiff (but not too dry).

2. When large bubbles begin to appear in the syrup (approximately 240°F), remove the syrup from the stove. Slowly pour the hot syrup in a steady stream while the egg whites are still beating. Add 2 teaspoons of vanilla. Beat for 2 to 3 more minutes.

Storage: Meringue Icing should be used within one day. It does not rebeat well.

Yield: 5 to 6 cups (1.2 to 1.4 L) or 2½ to 3 lbs (1.1 to 1.4 kg) icing

HIGH-YIELD YELLOW CAKE
LIGHT POUND CAKE

This yellow-cake recipe is based on Nick Malgieri's formula for large-volume baking. This recipe requires a 15- to 20-quart (15- to 20-L) mixer.

Ingredients
5 lbs (2.27 kg) cake flour
3 oz (84 g) baking powder
1 Tbsp salt
3 lbs (1.36 kg) unsalted butter, room temperature
6 lbs (2.72 kg) sugar
60 oz (1.79 L) whole eggs
2 fl oz (60 ml) pure vanilla extract
6 cups (48 fl oz or 1.43 L) buttermilk
4 cups (24 fl oz or 0.95 L) whole milk

1. Preheat oven to 325°F (163°C). Use vegetable oil spray on the top and sides of the 6-inch, 8-inch, or 10-inch (15-, 20-, or 25-cm) baking pans and line them with parchment paper. Set aside.

2. Add flour, baking powder, salt, and sugar into a large Hobart mixing bowl. Add sugar. Mix with a large paddle attachment until the mixture is combined. Cut up the soft butter* into large chunks and add to the flour mixture. Mix for 3 minutes.

3. Mix the vanilla, buttermilk, and whole milk.

Measure out 4 cups of the mixture and add to the flour-and-butter mixture. Mix on LOW speed for 3 minutes. Stop and scrape the bowl. Then mix on MEDIUM speed for 5 minutes.

4. Add the whole eggs, whisking them into the rest of the buttermilk-and-milk mixture. Add this mixture to the flour mixture in four turns, beating on LOW speed. Stop and scrape occasionally to make sure that the mixture is compeltely combined..

5. Ladle into cake pans, making them two-thirds full. Hit each pan against the counter to burst air bubbles (or pinprick them with a toothpick). Bake until the sides of the cake slightly shrinks and a toothpick inserted into the center comes out clean.

6. Depending on cake pan size, bake for 45 minutes to 1 hour.

* If you need to soften the butter, warm it slightly in a 250°F (121°C) oven until some of it melts a little.

Storage: This High-Yield Yellow Cake freezes well and can be stored for 2 to 3 months in the freezer.

Yield: sixteen 6x2-inch (15x5-cm) cake pans, ten 8x2-inch (20x5-cm) cake pans, six 10x2-inch (25x5-cm) cake pans, *or* three full sheet pans

PEANUT BUTTER CAKE

Children seem to gravitate to this nutty cake. Ice with Cream Cheese Buttercream or Amaretto Praline Mocha Buttercream for a delicious finale.

Ingredients
⅔ cup (170 g) butter, room temperature
½ cup (115 g) creamy peanut butter
1½ cups (345 g) granulated sugar
½ cup (115 g) packed brown sugar
3 cups (330 g) cake flour
1 Tbsp baking powder
1 cup (8 fl oz or 240 ml) milk
4 large eggs

1. Preheat oven to 350°F (175°C). Vegetable spray two 8-inch (20-cm) or one 10-inch (25-cm) cake pan (3 inches or about 7.6 cm deep). Line with parchment paper.

2. Cream together butter, peanut butter, granulated sugar, and brown sugar for 5 minutes. Stop and scrape the bowl. Cream for an additional 60 seconds.

3. Sift flour and baking powder together. Whisk together the whole eggs and milk.

4. Alternately add the flour mixture and egg-milk mixture to the batter in three turns. Mix until the batter is smooth. Spoon batter into prepared pans.

5. Bake for 45 to 50 minutes for 8-inch (20-cm) pans, and 60 to 70 minutes for 10-inch (25-cm) pans or until a toothpick inserted into the center comes out clean.

Storage: This Peanut Butter Cake lasts about 2 weeks in the refrigerator or 2 months in the freezer.

Yield: two 8-inch (20-cm) cakes or one 10x3-inch (25x7.5-cm) cake

1. Preheat oven to 350°F (175°C). Vegetable spray two 8-inch (20-cm) or one 10-inch (25-cm) cake pan 3 inches (7.5 cm) deep. Line with parchment paper.

2. Cream together butter, sugar, zest, lemon juice, and lemon curd for 5 minutes. Stop and scrape the bowl. Cream for 60 additional seconds.

3. Sift together the cake flour, baking powder, and salt. Mix in the shredded coconut. Whisk together the eggs, milk, and vanilla.

4. Alternately add the flour mixture and egg-milk mixture to the batter in three turns. Mix until the batter is smooth. Spoon the batter into prepared pans.

5. Bake for 45 to 50 minutes for 8-inch (20-cm) pans, and 60 to 70 minutes for 10-inch (25-cm) pans or until a toothpick inserted into the center comes out clean.

Storage: This Lemon Coconut Cake lasts up to 3 weeks in the refrigerator and freezes well.

Yield: two 8-inch (20-cm) cakes or one 10x3-inch (25x7.5-cm) cake

LEMON COCONUT CAKE

One of my favorite recipes, this is based on the moist yellow-cake recipe with other fun and delicious ingredients. It's a sure crowd pleaser whenever it is served.

Ingredients

1 cup (8 oz or 230 g) butter, room temperature
2 cups (1 lb or 454 g) granulated sugar
⅓ cup (80 ml) or 2.6 oz (75 g) Lemon Curd
2 Tbsp (1 fl oz or 30 ml) fresh lemon juice
zest of 3 lemons
3 cups (330 g) cake flour
1 Tbsp baking powder
½ tsp salt
1 cup (8 oz or 230 g) shredded coconut
5 large eggs
2 tsp vanilla
1 cup (8 fl oz or 240 ml) milk

CHOCOLATE CAKE CHEESECAKE

This totally decadent cake is extremely rich and moist. It's a sinful treat that requires a lot of preparation. If you can, make both the chocolate cake and the cheesecake the same day and refrigerate them for 24 hours. The cheesecake does not have a bottom crumb crush. Prepare the buttercreams in advance or on the day you plan to assemble this confection.

Ingredients

CHOCOLATE CAKE

1½ recipe Chocolate Fudge Cake

CHEESECAKE

32 oz (four 8-oz packages or 908-g) cream
    cheese, room temperature
½ cup (60 g) all-purpose flour
4 large eggs
14 oz (392 g) sweetened condensed milk
    (Eagle Brand)
2 tsp vanilla extract
1 tsp lemon extract

BUTTERCREAMS

½ recipe Cream Cheese Buttercream
½ recipe Chocolate Buttercream

For Chocolate Cake

Preheat the oven to 350°F (175°C). Vegetable spray two 10-inch cake pans and line with parchment paper. Follow the rest of the procedure for making the Chocolate Fudge Cake recipe on p. 142. Bake for 60 to 70 minutes or until a toothpick inserted into the center comes out clean. When cooled, remove from the cake pan, wrap in plastic wrap, and chill overnight.

For Cheesecake

1. Preheat the oven to 300°F. Use vegetable-oil to spray and line a 10-inch springform pan.
2. Cream the cream cheese for 5 minutes. Stop and scrape the bowl. Cream for 60 additional seconds. Beat in the flour. Add eggs one at a time to the creamed mixture.
3. Beat in the sweetened condensed milk, vanilla, and lemon extract and mix just until combined.
4. Pour into a prepared pan and bake for 60 to 70 minutes. Turn off the oven and let it rest in the oven for an additional 30 minutes with the oven door slightly opened. Remove from the oven and let cool. Chill overnight to develop the flavor of the cheesecake.

For the Buttercreams

Follow the recipes for Cream Cheese Buttercream and Chocolate Buttercream. (See recipes on pp. 136 and 137.)

To Assemble the Chocolate Cake Cheescake

1. Use a cake plate or foiled board. Trim the chocolate cake layers and cheesecake with a serrated knife, making sure that the layers are close in height and close to a 10-inch (25-cm) diameter.
2. Brush one chocolate cake layer with Godiva liqueur. Spread a little Cream Cheese Buttercream on the chocolate layer.
3. Carefully place the cheesecake on top of the chocolate cake. Make sure you remove the parchment paper under the cheesecake. Spread a little Chocolate Buttercream on top of the cheesecake, then, spread a little Cream Cheese Buttercream over the Chocolate Buttercream.
4. Place the second chocolate cake layer on top of the cheesecake. Brush with Godiva liqueur. Crumb coat all three layers with Chocolate Buttercream. Refrigerate for 1 to 2 hours. Ice smoothly with Chocolate Buttercream. Decorate the cake with your favorite buttercream piped borders.
Storage: Store the cake in the refrigerator. Eat the Chocolate Cake Cheesecake within 1 week.
Yield: three-layer cake with 10-inch layers

Fillings & Extras

LEMON or LIME CURD

This is a delicious cake or pie filling.

Ingredients
8 large eggs
2 egg yolks
1½ lbs (684 g) granulated sugar
zest of 10 medium-large lemons *or* limes
juice of 10 lemons *or* limes (for 12 fl oz or 360 ml juice)
1½ cups (¾ lb or 345 g) unsalted butter, cut into ½-inch (1.25-cm) pieces

1. Beat the whole eggs, egg yolks, and sugar together in a stainless steel bowl until well combined. Add lemon zest, lemon juice, and butter.
2. Cook in a double boiler over simmering water, stirring constantly until the curd starts to thicken (about 15 to 20 minutes). The curd is ready when it coats the back of a spoon. Strain immediately and cool over an ice bath.
3. Store the curd in a plastic container with plastic wrap directly on the curd. This prevents a skin on the curd. Cover with the lid. Refrigerate until ready to use.

Note: If 10 lemons or limes don't give you 12 fluid ounces (360 ml) of juice, squeeze more lemons and limes for more juice. If you wish, substitute oranges for the lemons or limes to create orange curd.

Storage: This Lemon or Lime Curd will last up to 2 weeks in the refrigerator. If you freeze it, the curd will last for 2 to 3 months.

Yield: 5½ cups

PINEAPPLE CURD

This is a refreshing change to lemon or lime curds. It's tangy and sweet.

Ingredients
8 large eggs
2 egg yolks
1½ lbs granulated sugar
1¼ cups (10 fl oz) unsweetened pineapple juice
4 oz chopped pineapple, fresh or canned
¼ cup (2 fl oz) fresh lemon juice
¾ lb unsalted butter, cut up and at room temperature

1. Beat the whole eggs, egg yolks, and sugar together in a stainless steel bowl until well combined. Add pineapple juice, chopped pineapple, lemon juice, and butter.
2. Cook in a double boiler over simmering water, stirring constantly until the curd starts to thicken (about 15 to 20 minutes). The curd is ready when it coats the back of a spoon. Strain immediately and cool over an ice bath.

Storage: Store the curd in a plastic container with plastic wrap directly on the curd. This prevents a skin on the curd. Cover with a lid. Refrigerate until ready to use or freeze for 2 months.

Yield: 5½ cups (1.3 L) or 2.7 lbs (1.2 kg)

SIEVED APRICOT JAM

This cake filling is easy to make, and it tastes great.

Ingredients
8 oz (224 g) apricot preserves
½ cup (4 fl oz or 120 ml) water

Cook the preserves and water together until they begin to simmer. Strain and allow the mixture to cool. Place it in a jar with a tight-fitting lid or use an airtight container. Refrigerate until ready to use.

Note: This recipe will work with any other kind of fruit preserve. Although we use preserves in this recipe, the water-added and sieved results is more properly called a kind of jam, hence our recipe title, Sieved Apricot Jam.

Storage: If refrigerated, the sieved jam will last for several months.

Yield: 8 to 10 oz (224 to 280 g)

SPACKLED PASTE

I invented this spackled icing paste to help perfect cake construction. This icing paste is delicious and unusual. People swear that they are eating a lovely nut filling.

Ingredients
3 to 4 cups (1½ to 2 lbs or 690 to 920 g) cake crumbs
½ to ¾ cup (120 to 180 ml) or 4 to 6 oz (115 to 170 g) Decorator's Buttercream
¼ cup (80 ml) or 2 oz (56 g) filling (citrus curd or preserve)

Mix the ingredients together to form a thick paste. If the spackled paste is too stiff to ice with, add more buttercream to soften the spackled paste or put ½ cup buttercream next to the spackle paste on an icing board. Use the buttercream to adjust the thickness of the spackled paste, or use water to help smooth the spackled paste onto the cake.

Storage: Use the Spackled Paste within 3 days.

Yield: Makes 2½ cups (600 ml) or 1¼ lbs (575 g)

BLOWN OR PULLED SUGAR

Blown or pulled sugar looks spectacular on cakes. Sometimes this recipe is simply called Isomalt sugar.

Ingredients
3 lbs (1.3 kg) Isomalt sugar
5½ tsp cold water

Special Equipment: silicone baking sheet (silpat), large marble slab, metal bars (for containing sugar), large metal spoon, bench scraper, bowl of cool water, 6- to 8-inch (15- to 20-cm) metal ring (for casting), good candy thermometer. If you don't have a silicone baking sheet, then lightly oil the marble slab.

1. Place the silicone baking sheet on the marble slab and arrange the metal bars on the silicone so that you have an enclosed rectangle that is as large as possible.

2. Melt the Isomalt in a heavy saucepan over LOW to MEDIUM heat. Using the metal spoon, occasionally press unmelted Isomalt pearls into the melted areas. When the Isomalt appears to be mostly liquid, stir with the spoon to distribute the remaining pearls evenly.

3. For casting, oil the inside of the metal ring with corn oil. Clean up the excess with a paper towel. Place a piece of aluminum foil under the metal ring and place the ring and foil on a silicone baking sheet. The aluminum foil gives a decorative design in the sugar piece once the sugar is cast and dried. Also, it protects the Isomalt syrup from seeping from under the ring as it dries.

4. Insert the candy thermometer and cook the Isomalt to 340°F (170°C). Watch the thermometer closely because the temperature rises very quickly. Once the correct temperature is reached, remove the pan from the heat and immerse the bottom of the pan in the cool water. This stops the Isomalt from cooking any further. Remove and dry the bottom of the pan.

5. Carefully add the measured water in two to three increments, stirring well after each addition. BE CAREFUL WHEN ADDING THE MEASURED WATER BECAUSE THE HOT SYRUP WILL BOIL UP.

6. If casting a disk for the blown balls, immediately pour some Isomalt sugar inside the oiled metal ring to about ⅛ to ¼ inch high. Let cool and set for 1 hour.

7. Carefully pour the remaining Isomalt syrup inside the rectangle formed by the metal bars. Let cool completely. This could take 20 to 30 minutes. Carefully remove one of the rectangle bars to see if the sugar has set.

8. When the sugar has set, cut the Isomalt sugar into 6 to 8 pieces with a bench scraper. Place a few pieces under a heat lamp for sugar blowing. The additional pieces when sufficiently cooled can be placed in a closed container with plenty of desiccant.

Storage: The unused Isomalt sugar can last for weeks or months as long as you store it in a tightly closed container with plenty of desiccant.

Yield: 3 lbs (1.3 kg)

GILDING

Gilding dresses up the simplest design in a most elegant way.

Ingredients
½ tsp powdered "gold"
2 to 6 drops lemon extract

Mix ½ teaspoon of powdered gold with a few drops of lemon extract. Stir with a small brush until you have a liquid solution. Use a sable paintbrush to brush on icing or cameos. When the alcohol evaporates, the gold turns into a solid. Add a few more drops of extract to convert it back into a liquid state.

Note: Unlike gold powder, gold leaf is actually 95.6% gold. This expensive decoration is quite edible.

Storage: Keep in a small container with a tight-fitting lid. The gilding will last indefinitely. To reconstitute the gold, add drops of lemon extract as needed.

Yield: This Gilding recipe makes enough to gild a large monogram or a 4-inch cameo mold.

Blown sugar balls can be colored to suit the design. They create a spectacular display on top of the cake.

Measurements

Finding the Perfect Measure

To achieve precise measurements and best results, many European professional pastry chefs weigh ingredients. While most American and Canadian home and professional bakers, chefs, and cake decorators rely on measuring cups and spoons, you may find that you achieve more reliable results if you weigh ingredients. Ingredient measurements can be critical to the success of cakes, icings, and fillings.

If you are familiar with certain ingredients and brands, and if you find that you achieve consistent results, then conventional American measurements may be just fine for you. However, we are aware that this book draws on cake-decorating techniques from around the world, and we hope that cake designers from five continents will want to find everything they need to know in one volume.

In most cookbooks, the conversion of standard U.S. measurements to grams and milliliters (in the metric system) are rounded off. Thus, 1 ounce, which is said to equal 28 grams, is actually 28.35 g. The 0.35 is rounded off or dropped to make the measurements less confusing and easier to manage. However, if you were measuring even a slightly greater volume or weight, such as 4 ounces, the equivalent would be 114 g, instead of the simple multiplication (28 g x 4 = 112 g). Here the 0.35 is refactored in; otherwise, you would lose grams that could be vital to the success of your recipe.

Of course, 2 grams would hardly effect the result of most cake or icing recipes, but in large-volume baking the accumulated weight difference in the desired weight or measurement of ingredients certainly could.

WEIGHING WITH A KITCHEN SCALE

Before you weigh the ingredient, first weigh the container you'll be using. Then turn your kitchen scale to "0" (zero), add the ingredient, and weigh again. Or, keeping your scale on true "0" (zero), simply deduct the weight of the container from that of the ingredient weighed in the container. For the most precise reading, use the gram weight.

FLOUR

When measuring flour in cake recipes, aerate the flour, folding it about ten times, with a wire whisk in a large bowl. Then dip the measuring cup into the flour. Use an offset metal spatula to level off the flour. When sieving or sifting the flour with baking powder or baking soda and salt, add the flour first to the bowl. Then add the rising agent and salt, if required. Whisk dry ingredients briefly and then sieve or sift.

10X Confectioners' Sugar

This is finely ground granulated sugar, which we commonly call confectioners' sugar or powdered sugar. The weight of 1 cup 10X con-fectioners' sugar is half the weight of 1 cup granulated sugar. It's best to use 10X rather than less finely ground (XXX or XXXX) con-fectioners' sugars.

Cocoa Powder

Cocoa powder weighs the same as flour or 10X confectioners' sugar. Sift it for the best results.

Measuring Cake Pans, Designing, and Piping

⅛ inch = 3 mm	2 inches = 5.1 cm (5 cm)	10 inches = 25.4 cm
¼ inch = 6 mm	2½ inches = 6.4 cm	11 inches = 27.9 cm
⅜ inch = 1 cm	3 inches = 7.6 cm	12 inches = 30 cm
½ inch = 1.3 cm	3½ inches = 8.9 cm	13 inches = 33 cm
⅝ inch = 1.6 cm	4 inches = 10.2 cm (10 cm)	14 inches = 35.6 cm
¾ inch = 1.9 cm	4½ inches = 11.4 cm	15 inches = 38.1 cm
⅞ inch = 2.2 cm	5 inches = 12.7 cm	16 inches = 40.6 cm
1 inch = 2.54 cm (2.5 cm)	6 inches = 15.2 cm	20 inches = 50.8 cm
1¼ inch = 3.2 cm	7 inches = 17.8 cm	22 inches = 56 cm
1½ inch = 3.8 cm	8 inches = 20.3 cm	24 inches = 60 cm
1¾ inch = 4.4 cm	9 inches = 22.9 cm	26 inches = 66 cm

Weight

¼ oz (ounce) = 7 grams (g)
½ oz = 14 g
1 oz = 28 g (28.35 g)
2 oz = 57 g
3 oz = 85 g
4 oz = 114 g
5 oz = 140 g (142 g)
6 oz = 170 g
8 oz = 228 g (224 g)
10 oz = 283 g (280 g)
12 oz = 340 g (336 g)
14 oz = 397 g (392 g or 400 g)
16 oz or 1 lb (pound) = 454 g
2 lbs = 908 g
2.2 lbs = 1 kg (kilogram)

Volume or Liquid Measurements

1 tsp (teaspoon) = 5 ml (milliliters)
1 Tbsp (Tablespoon) = 15 ml
2 Tbsp = ⅛ cup = 1 fl oz (fluid ounce) = 30 ml
¼ cup = 4 Tbsp = 60 ml
⅓ cup = 5 Tbsp + 1 tsp = 80 ml
⅜ cup = 6 Tbsp = 90 ml
½ cup = 8 Tbsp = 120 ml
⅔ cup = 10 Tbsp + 2 tsp = 160 ml
¾ cup = 12 Tbsp = 180 ml
1 cup = 16 Tbsp = 8 fl oz = ½ pint = 240 ml
2 cups = 16 fl oz = 1 pint = 480 ml
3 cups = 24 fl oz = 720 ml
4 cups = 1 quart = 0.95 L (liter)

Flour, Confectioners' Sugar, or Cocoa Powder

¼ cup = 30 g
⅓ cup = 40 g
⅜ cup = 45 g
½ cup = 60 g
⅔ cup = 75 g
¾ cup = 85 g
1 cup = 110 g
2 cups = 227 g
4 cups or 16 oz or 1 lb = 454 g

Granulated Sugar

Measure this sugar by weight or with a dry measuring cup. Level off the sugar in the cup with a metal offset spatula.

¼ cup = 55 g
⅓ cup = 75 g
⅜ cup = 85 g
½ cup = 115 g
⅔ cup = 150 g
¾ cup = 170 g
1 cup = 230 g
2 cups or 16 oz or 1 lb = 454 g

Other Dry Ingredients

Baking powder, baking soda, salt, and spices can be measured using a measuring spoon. Level off the dry ingredient in the spoon with a knife.

Butter, Margarine or Shortening

Measure butter, margarine, and shortening by weight.

¼ cup = 55 g
⅓ cup = 75 g
⅜ cup = 85 g
½ cup or 1 stick or 8 Tbsp = 115 g
⅔ cup = 150 g
¾ cup = 170 g
1 cup or 2 sticks or 16 Tbsp = 230 g
2 cups or 16 oz or 1 lb = 454 g

Eggs

Most recipes in this book call for large eggs. A large American-size egg with shell weighs about 2 oz or about 56 g. Without the shell, it weighs about 1¾ oz or almost 50 g. A dozen whole large eggs make 2⅓ cups (510 ml). A dozen large egg whites make 1½ cups (360 ml) egg whites. A dozen large egg yolks make ⅞ cup (210 ml) egg yolks.

For meringues, you'll want extra-large eggs. A whole extra-large egg with shell weighs about 2.25 oz or 63.8 g. A dozen whole extra-large eggs make 3 cups (720 ml). A dozen extra-large egg whites make 1¾ cups (420 ml), and a dozen extra-large egg yolks make 1 cup (240 ml).

For American eggs, AA, A, and B refer to the quality, with AA being the best. Other countries have their own rating systems. Of course, for your cake masterpieces, you'll want to buy the freshest and the best.

Corn Syrup and Molasses

Corn syrup and molasses can be measured with a liquid measuring cup; however, it's often hard to get all of the thick syrup out of the container. If you lightly spray the liquid measuring cup with a vegetable-oil spray, you can get almost all of the corn syrup or molasses out of the cup. These syrups are best measured by weight.

⅛ cup or 1 fl oz or 30 ml = 1½ oz or 42 g
¼ cup or 2 fl oz or 60 ml = 3 oz or 84 g
⅓ cup or 2.6 fl oz or 80 ml = 4 oz or 113 g
½ cup or 4 fl oz or 120 ml = 6 oz or 168 g
⅔ cup or 5.3 fl oz or 160 ml = 8 oz or 227 g
¾ cup or 6 fl oz or 180 ml = 9 oz or 255 g
1 cup or 8 fl oz or 240 ml = 12 oz or 336 g
2 cups or 1 pint or 16 fl oz or 480 ml = 24 oz or 672 g

LIQUIDS

Water, milk, and alcohol can be measured using a liquid measuring cup. You can measure large amounts of liqueur in a liquid measuring cup, too. Follow the Volume or Liquid Measurements guide on p. 153.

EXTRACTS OR LIQUEURS

Use measuring spoons for extracts, such as almond, vanilla, orange, or lemon, and for small amounts of liqueurs used in these recipes. Large amounts of liqueurs can use liquid measuring cups, just as you would for water or milk. See the Volume or Liquid Measurements guide on p. 153.

> ½ teaspoon = 30 drops
> 1 tsp = ⅓ Tbsp = 60 drops = 5 ml
> 3 tsp = 1 Tbsp = ½ fl oz = 15 ml

GEL AND PASTE FOOD COLORS

Gel food colors blend better than paste colors. Paste food colors came out first in the industry. Both are professional-strength food colors. You'll find them more intense than the food coloring available in most grocery stores. Use just a little food color on a toothpick. You'll need even less color when coloring a soft or creamy icing.

Temperature

In recipes, we give approximate temperature conversions from Fahrenheit (F) to Celsius or Centigrade (C). You may also need to adjust your oven or baking time if you live in a high altitude.

To convert Fahrenheit to Celsius:
> degrees F − 32 x 5/9 = degrees C

To convert Celsius to Fahrenheit:
> degrees C x 9/5 + 32 = degrees F

Water boils at 212°F (100°C) at sea level. At 2,000 feet (600 m), water boils at 208.4°F (98.4°C); at 5,000 feet (1,500 m) it boils at 203.0°F (95.0°C); at 7,500 feet (2,250 m) it boils at 198.4°F (92.4°C), and at 10,000 feet (3,000 m), it boils at 194.0°F (90.0°C). Note when making blown sugar balls.

Cakes baked at lower temperatures generally take longer to be done. Of course, a too hot oven will dry out or even burn a cake.

HIGH-ALTITUDE BAKING

For baking cakes in high altitudes, you'll need to slightly adjust the baking powder, sugar, and liquids, depending on how many feet or meters you live above sea level. You'll need to reduce the amount of baking powder and sugar and increase the amount of liquid.

ABOVE SEA LEVEL	BAKING POWDER REDUCE EACH tsp BY	SUGAR REDUCE EACH CUP BY	LIQUID FOR EACH CUP ADD
3,000 feet (900 m)	⅛ tsp	½ to 1 Tbsp	1 to 2 Tbsp (15 to 30 ml)
5,000 feet (1,500 m)	⅛ to ¼ tsp	½ to 2 Tbsp	2 to 4 Tbsp (30 to 60 ml)
Above 7,000 feet or (2,100 m)	¼ tsp	1 to 3 Tbsp	3 to 4 Tbsp (45 to 60 ml)

Piping & Embroidery Patterns

Copy the desired lace, curlicue, or other pattern at the desired size with a photocopier. Then use it as a guide beneath parchment paper for practice piping. For brush embroidery, pinprick the pattern on the cake and paint.

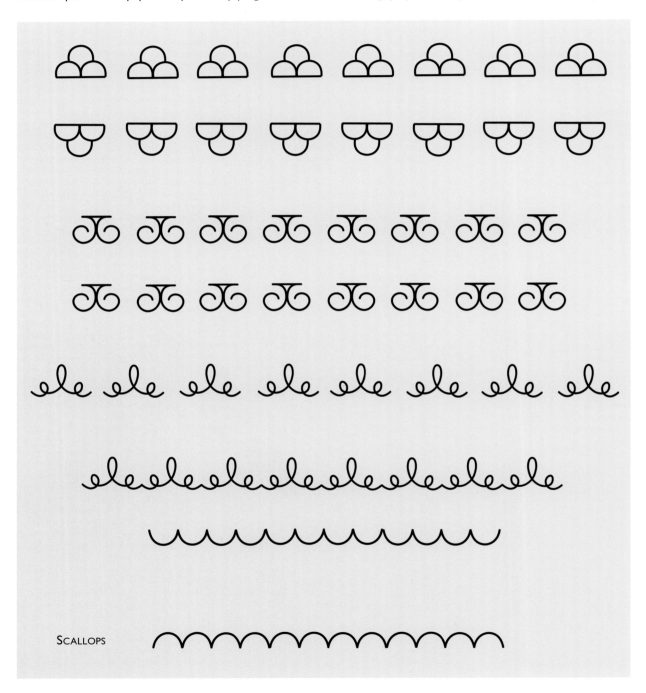

SCALLOPS

Cornelli Lace

Pinprick the pattern on the top of the cake to use for brush embroidery. (See p. 61.)

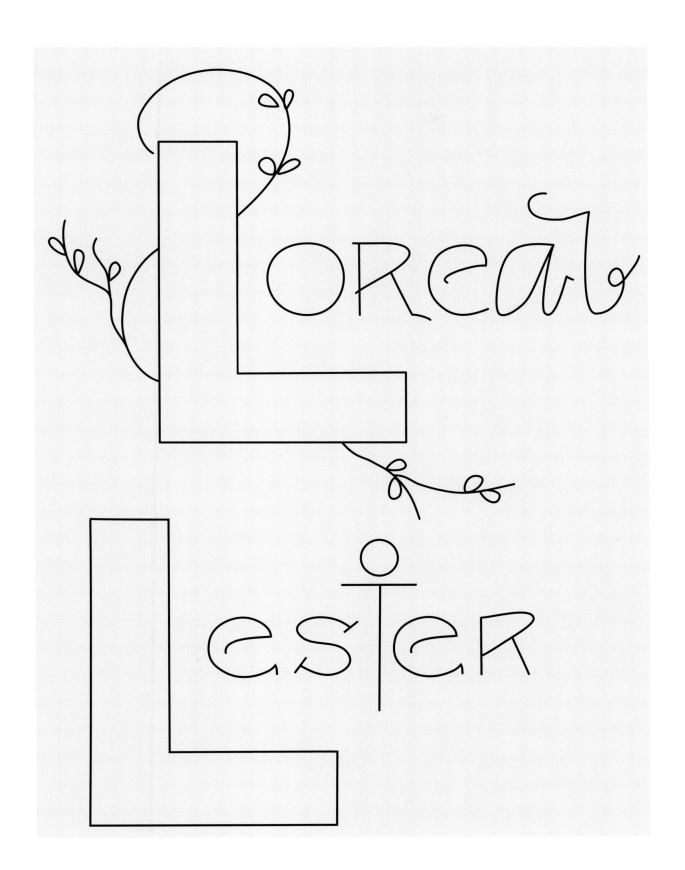

Monogram Lettering Guides

To create a monogram, photocopy the chosen letter(s) for the initials you want at the desired size. Put a piece of plastic wrap over the letter(s). Outline each letter in egg-white or meringue-powder royal icing, and then flood the letter in egg-white or meringue-powder flood icing.

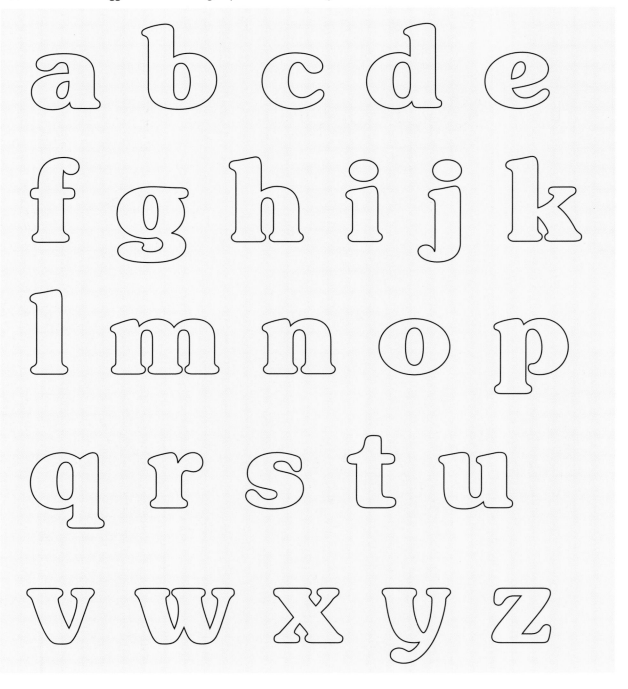

A B C D E

F G H I J

K L M N O

P Q R S T

U V W X

Y Z

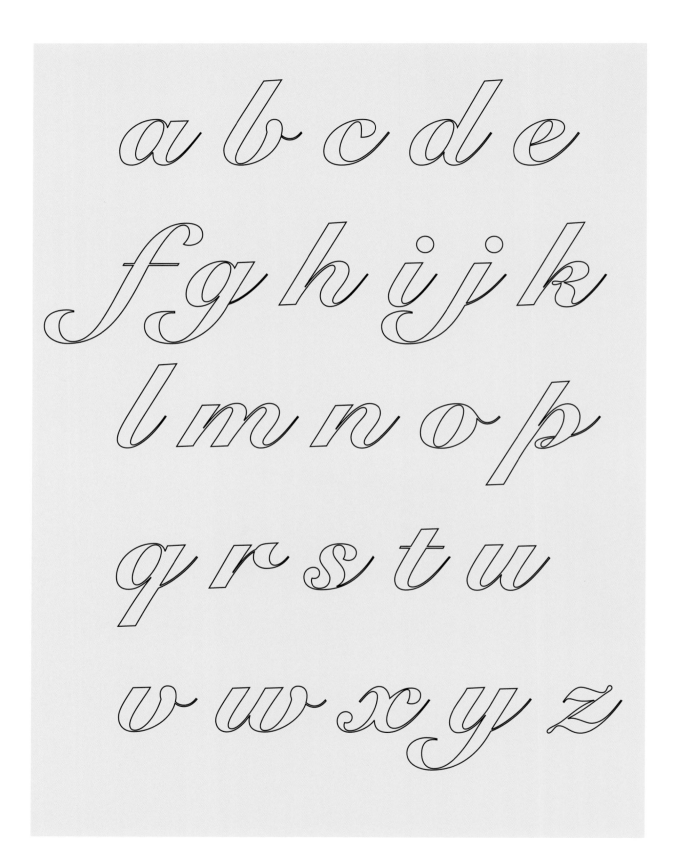

A B C D
E F G H
I J K L
M N O P
Q R S T
U V W X
Y Z

a b c d e

f g h i j k

l m n o p

q r s t u

v w x y z

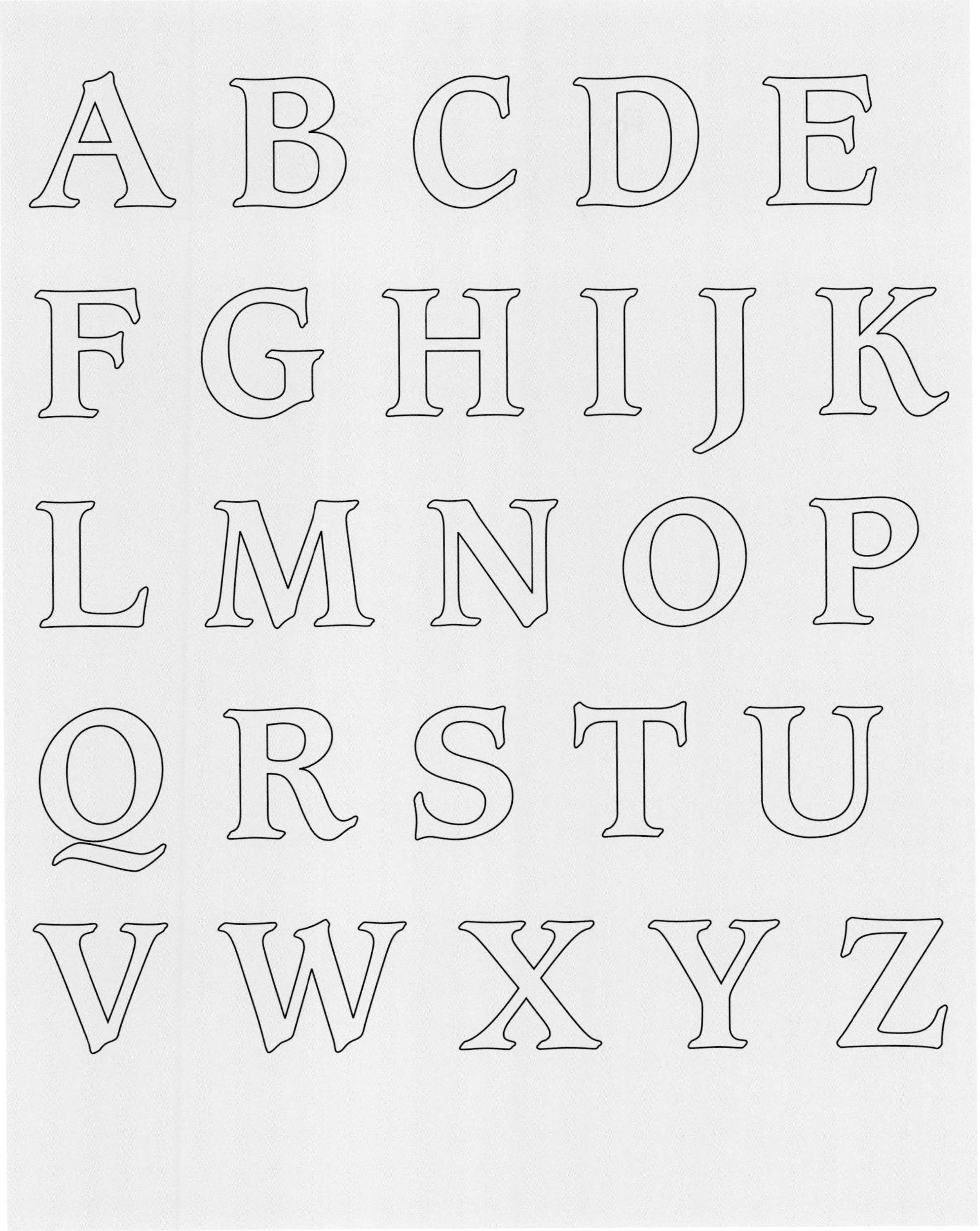

A B C D E
F G H I J K
L M N O P
Q R S T U
V W X Y Z

a b c d e

f g h i j k

l m n o p

q r s t u

v w x y z

A B C D

F G H I

L M N O

Q R S T

V W X Y

Special Cake-Decorating Supplies

You'll find most decorating supplies in your local kitchen, cake-decorating, or craft stores, or at cooking schools. A few hard-to-find products, such as Pettinice RTR Icing, Tylose (C), liquid whitener, gumpaste flowers, silicone molds, petal dust, and lace, rose-leaf, and tulip presses, are available only through specialty houses and distributors. We've listed these sources in the United States, Canada, England, Australia, New Zealand, South Africa, and Zimbabwe. Also check the Internet. You can access 1-800 toll-free calls within the United States and Canada. For suppliers in countries outside the United States and Canada, the country code is in parentheses followed by the city code and then the local phone number.

Albert Uster Imports
9211 Gaither Road
Gaithersburg, Maryland 20877
U.S.A.
Phone: 1 (800) 231-8154
Website: www.auiswiss.com
Isomalt sugar, pulled and blown sugar supplies, transfer sheets, chocolates, fillings, marzipan decorations.

American Bakels, Inc.
8114 South Hamilton Drive
Little Rock, Arkansas 72209
U.S.A.
Phone: 1 (800) 799-2253
Fax: 1 (501) 568-3947
Website: www.americanbakels.com
Pettinice RTR Icing distributor.

Annie's Cake Place
Shop 8
Crawford Center 166-168
Crawford Street
Queanbeyan, NSW 2620
AUSTRALIA
Phone: (61) 026 297-7190
Cake and baking supplies.

Beryl's Cake Decorating & Pastry Supplies
P.O. Box 1584
N. Springfield, Virginia 22151
U.S.A.
Website: www.beryls.com
Phone: 1 (800) 488-2749
Fax: 1 (703) 750-3779
Stencils, cutters, clay guns, textured rolling pins, Pettinice RTR Icing, Regalice Icing, cake-decorating tools.

The Broadway Panhandler
477 Broome St.
New York, New York 10013   U.S.A.
Phone: 1 (212) 966-3434 or
1 (866) COOKWARE
Website:
www.BroadwayPanhandler.com
Cutters, cake-decorating tools, stencils, textured rolling pins, commercial icings.

Cake Decorating Schools of Australia
Shop 7, Port Phillip Arcade
232 Flinders Street
Melbourne, VIC 3000   AUSTRALIA
Phone: (61) 039 654-5335
Cake-decorating and sugarcraft supplies.

Chipkin Bakery Supplies
174 Sutton Road
Sidwell, Port Elizabeth
SOUTH AFRICA
Phone: (27) 041 453-2976
Fax: (27) 041 453-6004
Bakery and cake-decorating supplies.

Cook's Dream, Inc.
8123 East Sprague
Spokane, Washington 99212
Phone: 1 (866) 285-2665
Fax: 1 (509) 924-0081
Website: www.cooksdreams.com
Cake-decorating supplies, cook and bakeware.

Creative Cutters
561 Edwards Avenue
Richmond Hill, Ontario L4C 9W6
CANADA
E-mail:
creativecutters@cakeartistry.com
Phone: 1 (905) 883-5638
Voice Mail or Fax: 1 (905) 770-3091
Gumpaste cutters, tools, presses, and classes.

Dee Sees Creations, Ltd.
P.O. Box 21
111 Flagstaff
Hamilton   NEW ZEALAND
Phone: (64) 07 854-3039
Cake-decorating and sugarcraft supplies.

Jem Cutters
P.O. Box 115
Kloof 3640   SOUTH AFRICA
1 Gray Place
Pinetown 3610   SOUTH AFRICA
Phone: (27) 31 701-1431
Fax: (27) 31 701-0559
New Jersey (U.S.A.) distributor:
1 (732) 905-0105
Fax: 1 (732) 886-9414
Website: www. Jemcutters.com
Tylose C, cutters, and tools.

Kitchen Collectibles
8901 J Street, Suite 2
Omaha, Nebraska 68127   U.S.A.
Phone: 1 (888) 593-2436
Website: www.kitchengifts.com
Copper cookie cutters.

New York Cake & Baking
56 West 22nd Street
New York, New York 10010   U.S.A.
Phone: 1 (212) 675-CAKE or
1 (212) 675-2253
Website: www.nycake.com
*Cutters, gumpaste tools, textured rolling
pins, clay guns, Pettinice RTR Icing,
presses.*

Orchard Products
51 Hallyburton Road
Hove, East Sussex BN3 7GP
ENGLAND
Phone: (44) 0127 341-9418
Sugarcraft cutters and tools.

Pattycakes, Inc.
34–55 Junction Blvd.
Jackson Heights, New York
11372-3828
U.S.A.
Phone: 1 (718) 651-5770
Fax: 1 (718) 533-8896
Website: www.pattycakes.com
*Cutters, bakeware, cookware, books, videos,
and cake-decorating and candy supplies.*

The Peppermill
5015 16th Avenue
Brooklyn, New York 11204   U.S.A.
Phone: 1 (718) 871-4022
Fax: 1 (718) 871-4025
*Kosher goods, Wilton products, bakeware,
cookware, cookie cutters, books, textured
rolling pins.*

Squire's Kitchen Sugarcraft
Alfred House
Hones Business Park, Waverley Lane
Farnham, Surrey GU9 8BB
ENGLAND
Phone: (44) 0125 271-1749
Website: www.squires-group.co.uk
Cake decorating and sugarcraft supplies.

**Sugar Bouquets by
Rosemary Watson**
23 North Star Drive
Morristown, New Jersey 07960
U.S.A.
Phone: 1 (800) 203-0629
Fax: 1 (973) 538-4939
*Lace presses, tulip presses, cutters, and
tools.*

Sugar Crafts N Z, Ltd.
99 Queens Road
Panmure, Auckland
NEW ZEALAND
Phone: (64) 09 527-6060
Cake decorating and sugarcraft supplies.

Sunflower Sugar Art, Inc.
2806 NW 72nd Avenue
Miami, Florida 33122   U.S.A.
Phone: 1 (305) 717-3103
Fax: 1 (305) 717-3175
*Lace, rose-leaf and gumpaste presses, petal
dust, and other tools.*

Surbiton Art and Sugarcraft
140 Hook Road
Surbiton, Surrey KT6 5BZ
ENGLAND
Phone: (44) 020 8391 4664
Fax: (44) 0870 132 1669
Website: www.surbitonart.co.uk
Cake-decorating and sugarcraft supplies.

**Sweet Inspiration Gum Paste
Flowers**
Division of Cal-Java International, Inc.
19519 Business Center Drive
Northridge, California 91324
U.S.A.
Phone: 1 (800) 207-2750
Website: www.cakevisions.com
Gumpaste floral sprays.

Wilton Enterprises
2240 West 75th Street
Woodridge, Illinois 60517   U.S.A.
Phone: 1 (800) 942-8881
Website: www.wilton.com
Baking and cake-decorating supplies.

Index

About the Author

Toba Garrett, master cake designer and sugar-craft artist, has studied the fine art of cake decorating with world-renowned chefs from England, France, Canada, Australia, New Zealand, South Africa, Mexico, and the United States. She attended Le Cordon Bleu in Paris. At the Institute of Culinary Education (the former Peter Kump's New York School of Culinary Arts) in Manhattan, she developed cake-decorating and confectionery-art curricula and teaches classes that are sold out months in advance.

In her remarkable career, Ms. Garrett has participated in many international exhibitions where her culinary excellence and artistry have enjoyed wide recognition. Her cake designs and decorated cookies have appeared in *Bride's, In Style, Gourmet, Essence, Showcase, Woman's Day, Chocolatier, American Cake Decorating, Pastry Art and Design,* and *Sugarcraft* magazines and in Bloomingdale's celebrity weddings showcases. Her wedding cakes have appeared in several books, among them Kate Manchester's *The Perfect Wedding Cake,* Maria McBride Mellinger's *The Perfect Wedding Reception,* and Bette Matthews's *Cakes for Your Wedding.*

Ms. Garrett has also been featured as a master chef and cake designer on television's "Emeril Live!" show on the Food Network, "B. Smith with Style" on MSNBC, "Our Home" with Bonnie Montgomery on Lifetime, "Home Matters" on the Discovery Channel, and other shows. Her culinary talents were celebrated on WOR-AM radio's "Food Talk," with Arthur Schwartz.

In 1996 she was one of eighteen master chefs chosen to create a showpiece for the 150th birthday celebration of the Smithsonian Museum in Washington, D.C. She has judged many culinary art shows, including the biennial Domaine Carneros Sparkling Wine Wedding Cake Competition.

Ms. Garrett has received many international awards, eight gold medals, six silver medals, three bronze medals, and dozens of diplomas and felicitations with distinction from culinary societies, such as the Amicale Culinaire de Washington, D.C.; Les Amis d'Escoffier; Les Dames d'Escoffier; the Saint-Michel; and the Société Culinaire Philanthropique de New York. In 1994 she won the Air France "trip to Paris" prize for wedding-cake designs. In 1996 she won the trophy of La Commanderie des Cordons Bleus de France for outstanding wedding-cake design. At the 1997 Salon of Culinary Art, she won the competition's highest award, a gold medal from Société des Chefs, Cuisiniers et Pattissiers de la Province de Quebec for outstanding wedding-cake design, and at the 1998 Salon of Culinary Art in New York, she won the 14-karat-gold medal-of-honor grand prize for pastry.

Ms. Garrett's first book, *Creative Cookies: Delicious Decorating for Any Occasion* (Sterling, 2001) has received accolades in *The Washington Post, The New York Daily News, Canberra Times,* and other publications.

She is a member of ICES, former president of the Confectionery Arts Guild of New Jersey, and former member of the British Sugarcraft Guild.

Ms. Garrett was educated at Fordham University and City College of New York in communications, theater, and fine arts. She has studied floral design at Parsons School of Design. She has a master's in educational and instructional technology from Long Island University.

641.8
  Gar

The well-decorated cake.

DEMCO